Young W
POETRY CO

GREAT MINDS

Your World...Your Future...YOUR WORDS

- Inspirations From The Eastern Counties
Edited by Aimée Vanstone

Young Writers

First published in Great Britain in 2005 by:
Young Writers
Remus House
Coltsfoot Drive
Peterborough
PE2 9JX
Telephone: 01733 890066
Website: www.youngwriters.co.uk

All Rights Reserved

© Copyright Contributors 2005

SB ISBN 1 84602 202 9

Foreword

This year, the Young Writers' 'Great Minds' competition proudly presents a showcase of the best poetic talent selected from over 40,000 up-and-coming writers nationwide.

Young Writers was established in 1991 to promote the reading and writing of poetry within schools and to the youth of today. Our books nurture and inspire confidence in the ability of young writers and provide a snapshot of poems written in schools and at home by budding poets of the future.

The thought, effort, imagination and hard work put into each poem impressed us all and the task of selecting poems was a difficult but nevertheless enjoyable experience.

We hope you are as pleased as we are with the final selection and that you and your family continue to be entertained with *Great Minds - Inspirations From The Eastern Counties* for many years to come.

Contents

Cecil Jones High School, Southend-on-Sea

Kylie Osborne (16)	1
Kayleigh Jones (15)	2
Elizabeth Hamlet (16)	2
Richard Marques (16)	3
Ashley Cutmore (15)	4
Louis Denholm (16)	4
Andrew Shute (15)	5
Daniel Baker (15)	5
Hollie Grace (16)	6
Michael White (15)	6
Nathan Priest (15)	7
Luke Cooper (16)	7
Christopher Smith (15)	8
Simon Comber (14)	8
Anthony Robinson (15)	9
James Cooper (14)	9
Rachel Murray (14)	10
Graham Lock (15)	10
Kerry Flower (16)	11
Paula Harman (16)	11
James Rooza (13)	12
Jason Simpson (14)	12
Beverley Cousinery (16)	13
Elizabeth Charles (13)	14
Chey Martin (15)	14
Tom Jarvis (14)	15
Ken Carlile (15)	15
Rachel Bartlett (15)	16
Matt Grobler (15)	17
Amie Byrne (15)	18
Shadi Hamta (15)	19
Adam May (16)	20
Alex Szukalski (16)	20
Lianne Riddell (15)	21
Chelsea Gallagher (14)	21
Hannah Aldridge (15)	22
Ike Aldridge (15)	23

Chesham High School, Chesham
Claire Huxley (12)	24
Danielle Edwards (11)	24
Grace Howell (11)	25
Claire Brosnan (12)	25
Jan-Michael McIntosh (14)	26
Hannah Gallant (16)	27
Alex Tatton-Brown (17)	28
Christopher Vincent (17)	29
Charlie Vale (11)	30

Cliff Park High School, Gorleston
Jonnie Bayfield (12)	30
Sarah-Louise Gee (13)	31
Sophie Dye (13)	31
Alex Durrant (13)	32
Holly Riches (12)	32
Chloé Ellis (13)	32
Vicky Barber (13)	33
Harry Yusuff (12)	33
Claire Tye (12)	33
Robyn Disbury (13)	34
Kieran Deeks (13)	34
Pierce Browne (12)	34
Ben Akerman (12)	35
Stephanie Willimott (13)	35
Samuel Malley (12)	35
Samantha Storey (13)	36
Joe Jones (12)	36
Jade Traves (13)	37
David Moore (13)	37
Mary Waters (12)	38
Lucinda Murray (12)	38
Shannon Carr (12)	39
Daniel Coates (12)	39
Christie Richards (12)	40
Emily Basey (12)	40
Sophia Nicholson (12)	41
Gemma Harlow (12)	41
Finola Young (13)	42
Faye Humphrey (13)	42

Kyle Watt (12)	43
Alex Wilkinson (12)	43
Sarah Harvey (12)	44
Peter Townshend (12)	44
Holly Tyler (12)	45
Julia Prettyman (13)	46

Gamlingay Village College, Gamlingay

Keziah Henley (13)	47
Jordan Macrow (12)	48

Kingsbrook School, Deanshanger

Jamie Taylor (12)	48
Daniel Lefevre (12)	49
Lucy Thorpe (12)	50
Awais A Saeed (11)	50
Adrian Alara (12)	51
Annie Thompson (12)	51
Lizzie Millidge (12)	52
Sarah Belmont-Colwell (11)	52
Max Ikin (13)	53
Rebecca Basketfield (11)	53
Taylor Willbond (13)	54
Mitchell Brown (12)	54
Clare Booth (12)	55
Felicia Gatenby (13)	55
Ollie Bishop (12)	56
Rebecca Houseago (12)	56
Chloé Moore (11)	57
Kieran Price (12)	57
Daniel Coll (12)	58
Danni Harris (12)	58
Thomas Taylor (12)	59
Joe Smith (12)	59
Sam Clarke (11)	60
Ross Lloyd (12)	60
Gemma Pullen (12)	61
Miles Luckett (12)	61
Emma Norman (13)	62
Peter Rhodes (11)	62
Nathaniel Nero (11)	63

Matthew Dimmock (12)	63
Helen Worrall (13)	64
Luke Gibbard (12)	64
Victoria Roberts (12)	65
Katie Arkle (13)	66
Francesca Boyle (13)	66
Amber Fox (12)	67
Leah Gay (13)	67
Rachael Urquhart (12)	68
Elisha Cowley (13)	68
Elliott Nichols (13)	69
Robbie McBreen (13)	69

Lonsdale School, Stevenage

Matt Taylor (18)	70
Martin Brassett (18)	70
Jo Brimson (16)	71

Lothingland Middle School, Lowestoft

Kai Dunn (13)	71
Jasmine Marsh (12)	72
Chloe Shields & Mia Taylor (12)	72
Adam Glover (13)	73
Thomas Broderick (12)	73
Vicky Howard (13)	74
Michelle McClean (13)	75
Cameron Gallagher (13)	76
Sherri Sawyer (13)	76
James Brabben (12)	77
Victoria Drysdale (13)	77
Jordan Kingsley (12)	78
Thomas Thorogood (12)	78

Lovat Middle School, Newport Pagnell

Emma Walton (11)	79
Greg Pape (11)	79
Lily Morris (12)	80
Emily Anderson (11) & Kathryn Myers (12)	81
Beth Lloyd-Jones (12)	81
Charlie Ball (12)	82

Chloe Cartwright (11)	82
Grace Finnigan (12)	83
Charlotte Heggie (11)	83
Ben O'Donnell (11)	84
Stephanie Lynes (11)	84
Matthew Sandall (12)	85
Paul James (12)	85
Milan Odedra (12)	85
Tara Smith (12)	86
Ryan Massey (12)	86
David Gaskell & Jack Overton (11)	87
Sophie Treslove (12)	87
Lynsey Dorn (12)	88
William Wimmer (11)	89

Mayflower County High School, Billericay

Sarah Maunder (14)	89
Melissa Newnham (13)	90

Onslow St Audrey's School, Hatfield

Kirsty Dyce (11)	91
Sam Adamson (12)	91
Brian Ratliff (12)	92
Laura Charalambous (11)	92
John Neicho (11)	93
Robert Walton (11)	93
Seamus Kerwick & David Chandler (12)	94
Adam Kyprianou (11)	94
Sara Ismail-Sutton (11)	95

Raunds Manor School & Sports College, Wellingborough

Adam Evans (12)	95
George Firth	96
Joseph Pickering (12)	96
James Hennessy (12)	97
Clare Cowling (12)	97
Lewis Chinnick (12)	98
Alex McLean (11)	98
Imogen Davis (11)	99
Oliver Buckley (12)	99

Ellis Snow (12) 100
Charlotte Simmons (12) 100

St Alban's Catholic High School, Ipswich
Natalie Johnson (12) 101
Bethan Sidoli (12) 101
Sam Richards (13) 102
Ruth Pope (13) 102
Louise Duffy (13) 103
Rachel Mulvey (12) & Jess Simpson (13) 103
Katharine Etheridge (14) 104
Jennifer McCarthy (14) 104
Leonie Guiler (12) 105
Natasha Crawley (12) 105
Polly Jackson (15) 106
Katie Piper (12) 107
Srilekhini Kadari (12) 108
Georgia Keogh-Horgan (16) 109
Shannon Veitch (12) 110

Stantonbury Campus, Purbeck
Jelani Blair (14) 110
Samira Sadiq (12) 111
Adam Billingham (13) 111
Atif Talukdar (14) 112
Natasha Davies (14) 112
Andrew Webb (14) 113
Eavan McFall (14) 113
Amy Myers (14) 114
Catherine Whitmore (14) 115
Cameron Akitt (15) 116
Stuart Atkins (12) 116
Richard Ackland (15) 117
Rachel Baker (13) 118
Heather Ross (13) 119
Alicia Perkins (13) 120
Mari Edwards (15) 120
Jack Chalmers (12) 121
Ashley Maycock (13) 121
Jake Bloomfield (13) 122
Paul Osborne (13) 122

Verishua Maddix (12)	123
Annette Nunn (13)	123
Katie Woodward (12)	124
Adrian Edwards (12)	124
Stephanie McKever (13)	125

Stoke-by-Nayland Middle School, Stoke-by-Nayland

Emily Bowman (11)	125
Olivia Stringer (11)	126
Jack Short (12)	126
Luke Wilding (11)	127
Jack Copping (12)	127
Michael Faulkner (11)	128
Andrew Carter (12)	128
Bill Younger (11)	129
Jack Clark (12)	129
Jack Anger (11)	130
Helen Clarke (11)	130
Katherine Brown (11)	131
Billy Richards (12)	131
Michael Boorman (12)	132
Fred Howe (12)	132
Lauren W & Charlotte O'Connor (11)	133
Olivia Powling (11)	133
Samantha Ingram	134
Naomi Welfare (11)	134
Catherine Chapman (12)	135
Sean Bocking & Harry Series (12)	135
Ella Etheridge & Rosie Coot (11)	136
Laura Moore (11)	136
Kerrie Boyes & Kristie Robinson (12)	137
Harriet Bourner (11)	137
Joseph Kurtz & Danny Hurlock (11)	138
Daniel McGuinness (11)	138
Calum Gilbey (11)	139
Kerrie Boyes (12)	139
Murray Cox (11)	139
Charis Boon	140
Connan Hammond (12)	140
Timothy Leach (12)	141
Eloise Warren (11)	141

Amy Young (12)	142
Georgia Drummond (12)	142
Warwick Marshall (12)	143
Freddie Brasted-Watts (11)	143
Molly Broughton (12)	144
James Hazell (11)	144
Maddie Lingi (11)	145
Hunter Wallis (11)	146
Matthew Haggett (12)	146
Alice Catchpole (11)	147
Kristina Elkin (11)	147
Florence Burdall Goodchild (11)	148
Chloe Chapman (11)	149
Ricci Powell (11)	150
Elliot Allan (12)	150
Leonie Dolling (12)	151
Jack Furssedonnc (12)	151
Christian Clarke (11)	152
Joseph Butcher (11)	152
George Killick (12)	153
Dean Riley (11)	153
Robbie Waters (12)	154
Lucy Ratcliffe (11)	154
Alice Dodd (11)	155
Alex Leon (11)	155
Ava Allan (12)	156
Georgina Howe (11)	156
Anja Donnellan (11)	157
Sophie Faulkner (13)	157
Ross Britcher (11)	158
Adam Todd (12)	159
Alex Stevens (12)	160
Lucy Cowlin (11)	160
Rhys Taylor (12)	161
Samantha Gammage (11)	161
Samuel Pentney (12)	162
Anthony Waugh (12)	162
Sam Faithfull (12)	163
Chris Heard (11)	163
Ashley Brandon (12)	164
Sam Trafford (12)	165

The John Bramston School, Witham

Natalie Sullivan (12)	165
Jade Markwell (14)	166
Jade Peters (14)	166
Hannah Gorrie (15)	167
Richard Clunie (14)	167
Amanda Green (12)	168
Darren Briley (12)	168
Patrick McDonagh (13)	169
Carl Walker (13)	169
Charlie Newman (13)	170
Michaela Williamson (13)	170
Rachel Challis (13)	171
Sadie Coe (14)	171
Danielle Williamson (13)	172
Rosie Sontag (13)	172
Daniel Sheehan (14)	173
Andrew Husband (13)	174
Warren Potgieter (14)	174
Warren Pennock (14)	175
Melissa Peckham (14)	175
Greg Cable (13)	176
Paris Smallbone (14)	177
Hayley Drew (14)	178
Ben Preca (14)	179
Rick Webb (12)	180
Dean Flowers (15)	180
Katie Hassain (12)	181
Jazmin Harrington (14)	181
Mathew Brown (15)	182
Kayley Ager (14)	182
Katie Hutton (12)	183
Kalvin Monk (15)	183
Daniel Cowell (13)	184
Yasmin Ledwell (14)	184
Katie Sage (15)	185
Christina Moore (13)	185
Charlie Jeffery (14)	186
Gemma Foxlow (12)	186
Rachael Hammond (14)	187
Sandy Rotondo (12)	187

Bethany Vale (12) — 188
Mark Brown (15) — 189
Corinne Fory (12) — 189
Jamie Wallace (12) — 189
Sarah Flood-Powell (15) — 190
Sam Field (13) — 190

The Leventhorpe School, Sawbridgeworth
Ruth Taylor (14) — 190
Holly Whitbread (12) — 191
Sian O'Connor (14) — 192
Amy Wilson (14) — 192
Charlotte Fereday (13) — 192
Bilal Mirza (13) — 193
Tom Buitenhuis (13) — 193
Georgia East (14) — 193
Vicki Lockwood (14) — 194
Joshua Horrax (14) — 194
Alex Plummer (14) — 195
Lucy Parker (14) — 195
Jamie Alison (13) — 196
Daniel Atkins (14) — 196

The Sweyne Park School, Rayleigh
Hannah Rawlinson (13) — 197
Georgia Vasa (12) — 197
Lilli Weekley (12) — 198
Luke Horton (13) — 199
Paul East (12) — 200
Sinead Pretty (13) — 200
Jasmin Wetton (12) — 201
Julia Sood (13) — 202
Li Sa Choo (12) — 203
Jade Ryan (12) — 204

Thurstable School, Tiptree
Laura Watkins (14) — 205
Sarah Baker (15) — 206
Zoe Willis (14) — 207
Rory Youngs (15) — 208

Carla Spenner (15)	209
Sian Fahie (14)	210
Paul Wilding (15)	212
Sophie Sheppard (14)	213
Taison Wade (15)	214
James Wren (14)	215
Daniel Hume (14)	216
Phillipa Casey (14)	217
Chris Webber (14)	218
Jessica Colegate (15)	220
Oliver Winn (15)	221
Sam Webb (14)	222
Jess Redfern (15)	223

The Poems

The Red Carpet

In the fields the poppies grow,
For miles around, row by row.

Men bent over, hunched were their backs,
Walking in line to the centre of attack.

Walking past the dead and hurt,
To the trench, full of dirt.

Armour, knives and guns at ready,
No one still, no one steady.

Eyes on targets, face to face,
Moving at a steady pace.

Prayers, screams and shouts so loud,
Men so scared, stood so proud.

Remembering they were the ones who tried,
To defend our country, side by side.

The struggle left so many dead,
A memorial place to lay each head.

Graves remain distant yet so near,
To remember those who were so dear.

Each grave surrounded by red flowers,
Who died within those tragic hours.

In the fields the poppies grow,
For miles around, row by row.

Kylie Osborne (16)
Cecil Jones High School, Southend-on-Sea

Thunderstorm Rage

As the radiant sunshine went behind the clouds
The wind took over, clouds bubbled in the sky
And all the rubbish is swept from the floor
Then violently thrown right into my eyes

As the sky starts to cry, flooding the earth
A storm rips through the sky
Forks of lightning stab into the ground
As people scramble to their homes

The lightning flashes as bright as sun
The rivers start to overflow
The thunder becomes more vicious by the minute
And booms ferociously and loud

The rain, like a waterfall, falling from the skies
The wind is a whirlpool, catching things inside
And into the night the storm drags on
Then in the morning the sun arrives.

Kayleigh Jones (15)
Cecil Jones High School, Southend-on-Sea

Summer Days

As I wander through the emerald green trees,
I see daisies, buttercups and busy bees.
The sun shines down upon the stream,
The leaves talk in the breeze it would seem.
As blue as the sky, the stream water flows,
Rushing down the hill it goes.
White fluffy clouds are blankets for the sky,
I stand and watch them float on by.

Elizabeth Hamlet (16)
Cecil Jones High School, Southend-on-Sea

Night's Rage

Shadowed by the jet-black sky
Standing all alone
Lightning jumps like a firefly
Trying to find its way home

Walking down a lonesome mound
I'm lost and want to be found
Nothing I can hear, but the sound
Of thunder all around

Shelter I must find
From this weather, cruel and unkind
I stumble like I'm blind
As the storm rages like it has no mind

Lightning strikes the floor
Fighting and wanting more
Thunder like a lion's roar
Animals flee in nature's war

This storm rages on and on
Unable to be stopped
Thunder explodes like a bomb
That has just been dropped

Weather calms after hours of storm
The sun shines down
Trees have been ripped and torn
Unknown of violence, the people of the town.

Richard Marques (16)
Cecil Jones High School, Southend-on-Sea

Right Vs Wrong

My mind is consumed in its own battle,
The constant battle of right and wrong,
But the wrong could be the right.

To fight is to maim and kill,
To not fight is selfish and cowardly.
We could die today or tomorrow,
We were lucky to survive yesterday.

Each time we kill, we draw close to Hell,
But can a meaningful prayer
Save us from eternal damnation?
What profit is there in a world full of death?

Ashley Cutmore (15)
Cecil Jones High School, Southend-on-Sea

Thunderstorm

The thunderstorm strikes at the sky
Like a million volts out of a plug
The colours are as black as a
Hungry wolf attacking its prey

The thunderstorm illuminates a town
Like a Christmas tree
But with the effect of a bomb scare

A sudden flash of fiery red
Disrupts the blackened sky shadows
Striking fear into the hearts of souls
Of everyone beneath.

Louis Denholm (16)
Cecil Jones High School, Southend-on-Sea

But

Nature is a beautiful thing
But yet it can be a destructive thing
It gives us rainbows and many colourful flowers
But can give us doom and gloom

Nature creates life
But can take it away
It gives birth to many wild and wonderful animals
But can create death in forms of natural disasters

Nature can create its own light show
But it can create its own horror show
It gives us the drama of lightning
But it also gives us the traumas of earthquake

Nature can be our best friend
But it can be our worst enemy
Nature can give us perfect weather
But nature can be pure evil.

Andrew Shute (15)
Cecil Jones High School, Southend-on-Sea

Lightning

The lightning fills the sky
Like a cataclysmic battle between gods
The bolts crash down
Punctuated by the blast of distant thunder
The blue fire creates a pattern of chaos
Across a pure black sky
As the cannon that is thunder
Blows deafening waves of unholy sounds
Clouds burst and unleash wave upon wave
Of ice-cold tears which slam into the ground.

Daniel Baker (15)
Cecil Jones High School, Southend-on-Sea

Taken In Vain

Life can be taken in the harshest way,
Alive by night and dead by day.

As you stand on the field with a gun in hand
And voices freeze across the land,

Your heart like a drum to you sounds loud,
As you stand eyes open, tall and proud.

Your friends and family at home, they prey,
As your life can be taken any day.

You stand, you're shot and die in pain,
To know your life was taken in vain.

Hollie Grace (16)
Cecil Jones High School, Southend-on-Sea

Natural World

It's growing from beneath the crust
Filled with Mother Earth's burning blood
Pressure's growing day after day
It's a future death machine
Mighty tall and super strong
An uncontrolled titan
When it releases its amazing power
Beauty and strength are quickly released
In a massive roar -
Murdering what's left of the old
In a single wave.

Michael White (15)
Cecil Jones High School, Southend-on-Sea

Harmony To Havoc

The birds sing in harmony
As the morning sun rises to greet the waking land.
The vegetation comes into Genesis
As dew rises into the crisp clouds.

Animals engage in peace,
As if Pandora's box had never been opened.
Slowly these ways of life begin to die
As a killing force enters the world . . .
Man.

Nathan Priest (15)
Cecil Jones High School, Southend-on-Sea

World War I

They trudge along the trenches deep,
All cold and damp and half asleep.
A man-made star lights up the sky,
They wonder who's the next to die.

The shells explode and bodies break,
The noise is such - the dead awake.
A voice shouts out, 'What's this for?
Why are we in the goddamn war?'

In the mud his body lies,
Now only food for the flies.
A waste of life, that we all know.
It wasn't really his time to go.

Luke Cooper (16)
Cecil Jones High School, Southend-on-Sea

The Sea

In the sea you can have lots of pleasure,
Swimming, diving, and looking for treasure.
Engulfed in the sea that is so vast,
Are many ships from the past.

Its mood changes from calm to rough,
So sailing a boat can be quite tough.
The bottom of the sea is hidden in black,
For what lives down there, is the knowledge we lack.

The colour of the sea changes a lot,
Depending on what's in it, and what's not.
A lot of emotions the sea does show,
It can be your friend, or even your foe.

Underwater creatures, in the sea they thrive,
If we stay down too long, it'll claim our life.
Half of the world is taken by sea,
For wherever it is, it's its own property.

Christopher Smith (15)
Cecil Jones High School, Southend-on-Sea

The World

I knew the world was horrible when it was born,
Since then, millions of years ago,
It shattered and crumbled to my feet.
I try and use my voice,
To calm and soothe the ugly world's voice,
It makes the world feel more comfortable.
For me, I have no choice but to die on Earth,
Or to try and communicate in the world's way.
I never cared about the sound of the world's fury and hatred,
But what hurts me the most
Is the world's hate is eternal.

Simon Comber (14)
Cecil Jones High School, Southend-on-Sea

In Hell

Bullets fell like the rain on an autumn night,
Fires far off light up the sky.
Men cried, shouted, screamed in fright,
They're in Hell willingly, prepared to die.

Blood and mud and gore and sweat,
Carpeted the floor and poisoned the scene.
A place like this, these men have never met.
Explosions made lights, that flew in beams.

A minute - a day, a day - a year,
The war lasted forever.
The men couldn't escape, not even in beer.
Days long and awful, even the weather.

War affects everyone, even the children,
Families separated, forever, for years,
'Will he be home soon?' worries the family,
But he lies dead, slaughtered like deer.

Anthony Robinson (15)
Cecil Jones High School, Southend-on-Sea

The Natural World

Wildebeest and zebras' tails flicking at flies,
Grazing in herds on the Serengeti plains.
Sun beating down from cloudless skies,
Rivers still full from the annual rains,
Whales in the oceans, fish in the lakes,
Monkeys swinging high in the trees,
Amazon rainforests full of insects and snakes,
Bright coloured flowers attracting the bees,
All kinds of animals we love so much,
This wonderful world, we must not touch.

James Cooper (14)
Cecil Jones High School, Southend-on-Sea

The Sea

My wispy blue splashes
Lap against the grass-green shores.
Calming, soothing,
Angry, threatening,
My tranquil sheet of beauty.

I can be angry,
I can be calm.
I can be warm and cold,
My oceans, my seas,
My tranquil sheet of beauty.

I can get angry when storms come,
I can get warm when the sun comes out
From behind them dark, gloomy clouds.
Little objects floating round in my bottomless stomach,
My tranquil sheet of beauty.

Rachel Murray (14)
Cecil Jones High School, Southend-on-Sea

The 'Noble' Chase

Paws pound and tail swishes,
Running past all hopes and wishes.
Fat chasers suck cigars and port,
As they pursue a 'noble' sport.
Dodge round trees and slip the trap,
Try to elongate the gap.
Urge the dogs and blow the horn,
'It will wish it was never born.'
The hounds close in and stop the 'beast'
And, with barks of joy, they feast,
While humans look upon the dead,
Tell me, which is the animal in red?

Graham Lock (15)
Cecil Jones High School, Southend-on-Sea

World!

Where mice scuttle in the field,
Where owls perch low, waiting,
Where rivers run clear and clean
And trees grow tall and flowers bloom,
A world I dream,
My one dream world.

Where towers big, bold, blocking out light,
Where water needs filtering
And trees stopped in their path; dead,
Where homeless animals roam the streets,
A world I know,
Heal my world, heal the world.

Kerry Flower (16)
Cecil Jones High School, Southend-on-Sea

Silent Dreams

A silent dream of your mind,
A dream until the nightmare starts,
A soft caress of twilight stars,
A piercing knife across your heart.

The crying eyes see not the truth,
The shards of a broken mirror fall,
The reflection of a hidden place,
The beginning of an endless call.

A burning passion of your soul,
A fire deep within your eyes,
A stolen power haunts your days,
A desperate plea for hidden lies,

Your inner beauty grasps the night.

Paula Harman (16)
Cecil Jones High School, Southend-on-Sea

Ode To The Natural World

Big or little, great or small,
Standing still or posed to crawl.
Ode to the world and all that it bares,
From cats and dogs to ants and hares.

Strong or weak, fierce or tame,
Creatures or plants with the weirdest names.
Everything that lives on Earth,
Ending in death and beginning in birth.

So remember when you're lying in bed,
The thousands of thoughts flying through your head,
Always think what put you there . . .
Ode to the natural world!

James Rooza (13)
Cecil Jones High School, Southend-on-Sea

Snowy Day

There was snow everywhere
It was freezing cold
There were people having snow fights
Young and even the old

There was ice on the lakes
There was snow on the roads
There were people having fun
But I was alone

Nobody liked me
I was the geek of the town
I wished I could go out
But I wasn't allowed

I was waiting for the snow to go
Why can't it be today?
So I could be allowed out to have fun
And finally play.

Jason Simpson (14)
Cecil Jones High School, Southend-on-Sea

Unanswered Questions

Where does one turn, when one's life has faded to the fact that friends,
Family and partners have become very distant?
Why do we feel insecure, when we watch the love of our life
Walk away from us, with someone else?
Why do we suffer in silence, when our hearts are breaking to the core?
Why do we not find the words to say to justify our actions
And why do we sit back and watch events happen that tear our hearts
To shreds, when we know we can stop them from happening?
This trip consisted of all these whys!
When does one decide to give up their life with civilisation
And cocoon themselves in their own world where paranoia,
Insecurities and heartache is all that is known?
Do we ignore the ones who need us the most?
Are we oblivious to the ones who are crying within themselves
And the only people that can hear their cry are banshees
Do we not understand the pain of those who live in their world
Of betrayal and heartache?
Questions are yet to be answered!
But from whom do we retrieve our answers?
Insecurities and uncertainties build in increasing amounts,
Until one decides life is not for them.
Until we feel life cannot provide us with everything we desire, except
Bitter endings, feuds, disappointments and heartache!
Do we decide who lives or dies?
Do we struggle through life as if life is a hurdle that must be overcome
And then death is our reward? Our rest? Our relief from life's pains?
Our resting place, where nothing can touch or destroy us?
Is death the answer to one's problems?
No more hurt. No more lies. No more disappointments
And best of all, no more life!

Beverley Cousinery (16)
Cecil Jones High School, Southend-on-Sea

Brown Labelled Girl

The little girl stands nervously at the door
Touching the brown label round her neck
Hugging her teddy bear close to her

She looks back sadly at the home she is to leave
Her grandmother standing at the window
Dabbing away the tears

Her dad already gone away in a foreign land fighting
Her mum hugs her tight as tears roll down her sad face

The coach pulls up full of children, but oddly quiet;
The little girl gives her mum one last big hug and kiss
Then climbs aboard still hugging her teddy tight.
She waves goodbye as the coach pulls away.

Yes, war has claimed another victim.

Elizabeth Charles (13)
Cecil Jones High School, Southend-on-Sea

Killer Weather

The booming thunder rolled
Across the dark foreboding sky
The air is icy cold
And the mist hides the pale moon

The stars blazed like a fire
Lighting the inky midnight dark
They shone delivering dire
Warnings across the sapphire velvet

The raging wind tears
Through the ongoing night
It stops and stares
Nothing left in sight

Darkness falls and all is still
Lightning strikes terror as if to kill!

Chey Martin (15)
Cecil Jones High School, Southend-on-Sea

Forest Fire

After two weeks without rain, plants begin to die.
The ground fries under the burning sun.
First a leaf starts to smoke,
Then a yellow flame appears,
That burns the nearest thing.

Then a bush is consumed, then a tree
And soon panicking animals begin to flee.
The whole forest burns with a hellish glow.

After weeks, the fire is done,
Leaving a dust as black as death.
But in the end, nature will triumph,
As soon sprouts begin to grow,
Ready for nature to thrive again.

Tom Jarvis (14)
Cecil Jones High School, Southend-on-Sea

Awake Me Not

Walking along, with the tumbling leaves,
Urged along with a gentle breeze.
I stop to rest and to see,
What it is that surrounds me.
So leave me be
And let me stay;
Awake me not
From where I lay.

Sprawled out, with the grass as my bed,
I begin to process the visions in my head.
The hustle and bustle of the real world behind;
I close my eyes and silence my mind.
So let me be
And leave me sound;
Awake me not
From this beauty profound.

Ken Carlile (15)
Cecil Jones High School, Southend-on-Sea

Thunderstorm

The sky as Delphic as coal
As the clouds drift towards me
I stand there in the freezing cold
The wind blowing against my cheeks
My face as cold as ice
Every second now the sky is looking more
Mysterious than before

All of a sudden I jump with fear
As a loud bang appears
The lightning comes
I'm all alone
Standing in the street
Everyone's screaming
Everyone's rushing to get into their homes

The lightning's bright
It hurts my eyes
I stand and stare at the empty road
Just me on my own
The wind is getting stronger
I can't hold out much longer

I walk away slowly
From the fantastic thunderstorm
The wind is blowing
The lightning is flashing
The thunder still banging
That's the fantastic
Thunderstorm.

Rachel Bartlett (15)
Cecil Jones High School, Southend-on-Sea

Lightning Strikes

Eager, I scan the darkened sky
And see the swirling clouds above,
Obliterating light of stars
But creating a new light of love.

The wind blows stronger, my heart beats
To know a storm is coming fast -
I smell it on the freshening breeze,
Hope this one's wilder than the last.

I throw my face into the wind,
To taste the sharp metallic bite
Of electric current, rushing around,
Knowing this will be a sight.

I shed my clothes, feel sting of rain,
Cold and cleansing, I step out
To have it drench me, spread my arms,
It feels so good, I start to shout.

But it out-shouts me with its force,
As energy bolts from the earth
And blazes to the sky above,
This must be like the edge of birth.

An instant etching on the dark,
A booming cannon in my ears,
A strike! Close! Might make me deaf,
The moment brings me close to tears.

It's amazing, it scares me not,
It's Earth and nature in true form.
I'm never chilled when lightning strikes,
In fact, it makes me feel quite warm!

Matt Grobler (15)
Cecil Jones High School, Southend-on-Sea

Storm

I feel I'm drowning in this storm
The more I fight, the harder it is to be calm
If I could just forget, everything might be alright
Losing my strength with all these sleepless nights

If there wasn't such a thin line
Between the love and hate that is yours and mine
Can't you hear the screams that I cry?
I'm drowning in these waves yet my mouth is so dry

When I can see you
Everything becomes alright
If you were there so I could see you
The darkness in my eyes would turn to light

I will never walk on water
Because you'll never be there to break my fall
All the times I've gotten to the surface
I just sank back down because I couldn't see your face

If I could just forget the ways you made me feel
Erase all my pain and start over so everything's healed
If I could just forget
Then maybe everything would be alright.

Amie Byrne (15)
Cecil Jones High School, Southend-on-Sea

Magnificent Mother Nature

I am the glorious sun, rising with each new day,
I am the magic of winter turning to spring.
I am the spider's web dripping with dew, crystals dancing
　　　　　　　　　　　　　　　　on the fine thread.
I am the birds which fly south, always returning.
I am the mighty lion pouncing on its prey.
I am the first rays of sunlight after the storm,
I am the huge waves crashing against the rocks.
I am the beautiful butterfly - its delicate wings outstretched.
I am the rainbow arching across the sky,
I am the long grass whispering secrets.
I am the swan gliding gracefully across the looking-glass lake.
I am the erupting volcano, molten lava running down my sides.
I am the millions of young turtles making their first journey
　　　　　　　　　　　　　　　　to the ocean.
I am the Swiss mountains concealing the 'ice man' for
　　　　　　　　　　　　　　　　thousands of years.
I am the Canadian redwood, who knows how high I will grow?
I am the endangered panda, the soft summer rain,
The smell of damp earth, the deadly python,
The caterpillar forming a chrysalis.
I am, I am,
The magnificent Mother Nature.

Shadi Hamta (15)
Cecil Jones High School, Southend-on-Sea

Beauty And Corruption

Lighting the sky in neon blue,
The pulsating electricity all night through.
As the roaring thunder descends from overhead,
Each second passes, another victim dead.

Its power and capabilities go unforeseen,
Unstoppable and overpowering
Against man's greatest machines.
Like an untamed beast roaring through the night,
Like a championship boxing match,
A twelve-round fight.

After chaos and corruption, the pictures are seen,
The morning after - a most beautiful scene.
They say a picture paints a thousand words,
The storm paints pictures, many absurd.
This most beautiful disaster has taken its turn,
On a series of events in our natural world.

Adam May (16)
Cecil Jones High School, Southend-on-Sea

Surfer's Dream

As the clean swell crests,
Swarming the coast of every land,
Each tube, spray, outbreak,
Sweeps infinite beauty upon the sand;
Our field of vision, ever changing thick and fast.
The build-up advances, smooth and glassy,
Then shatters and sprays until the next.

As the winds uprise and the swell amplifies,
Tension between us, our crowd, our friendship,
Waiting to join our nature, our world,
Explodes - scorching the fresh spray.
Yielding our tool, the creation within,
To fuel our passion, outside and in.

Alex Szukalski (16)
Cecil Jones High School, Southend-on-Sea

Thunderstorms!

Darkness fills the sky,
As the rain walks by.
Lightning flashes,
As thunder crashes.
My whole day passes by.

Rain smashes against my window,
As the sky becomes a widow,
Emptiness fills the air,
As people look out and stare,
The world is a shadow.

Sadness overcomes me,
As death stalks the sky.
I look towards tomorrow,
Instead of concentrating on the sorrow,
My family comforts me.

Lianne Riddell (15)
Cecil Jones High School, Southend-on-Sea

Winter's Night

Howling wind crept
Through the whispering wood,
Thick black clouds covered the dreary sky
Like a blanket.
Frosty leaves
Falling in the night sky
Bleak and bare trees shivered
Against the frozen stream
Whispering birds
Crying wolves
Hiding in the dismal cold storm.

Chelsea Gallagher (14)
Cecil Jones High School, Southend-on-Sea

The Natural World Of Thunder

Merging with traffic,
To escape the hailing rain,
Terror and anxiety,
Down the long country lane.

Overpowering, uncontrollable,
Strikes of forked lightning,
Like a whip upon bare skin,
Ongoing and frightening.

Panic-stricken community,
Running for cover,
Searching for shelter,
From this storm, like no other.

Sitting anxiously in this small enclosed car,
Rain-like tears from someone who cries,
Claustrophobia oppressing my thoughts and actions,
Why won't this stop? This storm certainly isn't shy.

The thunder sounds like a lion,
Growling angrily at its prey,
Thunder like a funeral bell,
I hope this stops soon . . . I pray.

Hannah Aldridge (15)
Cecil Jones High School, Southend-on-Sea

The Forest Fire

From my small house, overlooking the forest,
I noticed a colossal, gigantic smudge
Of thick swirling black smoke.
It was coming from the great forest itself,
The temperature was blistering,
The heat was immense.

I could see the fire flickering its flames,
Licking every tree standing by.
As the trees burn, a thick, strong smell
Of burning bark reaches my nostrils.
My lungs choke . . .

The roaring of the fire is overpowering,
Letting anybody know that it's not going to stop.
The fire lively, energetic,
The sky is a blotch of black ink,
Touching the tips of every mountain.

The loud sound of two helicopters' propellers can be heard,
A tidal wave of water comes rushing from the sky
And hits the heart of the fire.

Sirens ring across the landscape,
The forest fire leaves its mark
Of black, warm ash across the forest,
Scattered everywhere.

Ike Aldridge (15)
Cecil Jones High School, Southend-on-Sea

I Sang The Song Of Rainbows

I sang the song of rainbows and I painted with the stars
I rode on the back of the wind and I sailed in a car
I swam across the sky and I flew into the sea
I swallowed boiling magma and washed it down with tea
I ran around the world and I skipped to Timbuktu
I bought a leather necklace and I wore a diamond shoe
I tunnelled through a mountain and I raced with a bear
I hunted for a phoenix and I found a dragon's lair
I swapped a bag of gold for a tiny magic bean
I sunbathed with a snowman and I dined with a queen
I read a thousand poems and I wrote a thousand more
I won a prize for peace and I tried to stop a war
I froze inside a fire and I fought with a crook
I tangoed with the words when I danced with a book
I spent many hours eating strawberry ice cream
Then I woke from my sleep and I left the land of dream.

Claire Huxley (12)
Chesham High School, Chesham

Family

My family is who I love the most,
The ones that I trust from coast to coast.
When times are rough,
When times are tough,
They're always there for me.
If a tear comes, Mum'll wipe it away,
If you need help, Dad'll make it OK.
My family is who I love the most,
The ones that I trust from coast to coast.
Holidays, friends and enemies come and go,
But your family are there when your feelings are high and low.
They stay with you forever,
Forever you are together.
My family is who I love the most,
The ones that I trust from coast to coast.

Danielle Edwards (11)
Chesham High School, Chesham

The Hunter

The dark cold night on a moonlit moor
Shines terror and fear, that's for sure
He's everywhere, far or near
Beware, beware, the hunter is here

His victims are unpredictable
You're gone without a doubt
The bloodthirsty killer of innocent souls
Could choose you next, so watch out!

One weakness that shows to all the world
Is his fatal fear of light
It burns his flesh with a sizzle and crackle
That's why he hunts at night

The warm glow of the sun is here
Our killer can't go on
He disappears off with the morning mist
No fear, no fear, the hunter is gone . . .

Grace Howell (11)
Chesham High School, Chesham

Evening Of Emotion

Looking out through my window
My twisted day draws to an end
But my thoughts are still a wondering
My shattered dreams
Are hard to mend

The sunlight's fading swiftly but slowly
Like sand falling down through a timer
There's an emotional mountain in front of me
But I'm afraid I'm not a climber

What's left of the sun forms shadows
With branches, like ropes
The desperate light clings onto those branches
Like me, clinging onto my hopes.

Claire Brosnan (12)
Chesham High School, Chesham

Ignorance Is Bliss

I walk your corridors, cold and alone,
My name is unspoken, unheard, unknown.
Faces stare and laugh,
As I slowly walk past,
Head pointed to the ground
And my face carries a frown.
I hear you start to hiss,
But ignorance is bliss.

Because of my colour I must take your blame,
Feeling like Christ, enduring His pain.
You stare and whisper as I sit down,
All around me is that high chattering sound.
I open my books and try to learn,
But your ever-present stares begin to burn,
To churn all the anger up inside of me,
Tears build up, do you not see?
Your insults are not subtle enough to miss,
But of course, ignorance is bliss.

I try to play your sports,
As best as I can,
No teamwork, not even a helping hand.
You push me down and curse at me,
Is this how brothers are supposed to be?
Can this go away with one tender kiss
Or will ignorance always be bliss?

I hide from you, in the only safe place there is,
Behind my hands I try and escape your fists,
That you throw at my head, my legs, my chest.
Is it supposed to be like this
Or is ignorance of course, just and will always be, bliss?

Jan-Michael McIntosh (14)
Chesham High School, Chesham

Holding Your Light Before My Path

Something as easy in pain of trial, as dew upon fresh morning feet
When two souls from distance, o'er dark land, meet.
Wisdom in your mind, love betray your lips
And your hunger for the truth of me, gave my life some scope:
From thus above your bespectacled face
Hung wintering eyes of hope
And beyond the childish, smitten hands;
A soul so full of grace.
Yet in mine heart too desolate,
You buried a love so delicate
That only you may embrace it
And only we may know it.
There to be; untouched and growing
Day by day for evermore,
In lusting frames; in tending hands.
Not with you, it's too cherished:
In your heart's treasure chest,
So many things beyond mere chattels
That I may not even have begun to explore, lest
You might have not fallen for me.
But now, you've not only given into mine, your door,
Not a glass through which I can just wish of and only hope to see,
But your own true exposure laid out for me to tend.
And in return, you have the strangest want,
For my heart, with your love to mend.
Complain I of this obscurity?
To the contrary, I hold this honour dear,
For it means far more than, how to laymen, it might be portrayed.
It is beyond all explanation, how vital it is
To simply know you hold close my heart, and I too,
Keep yours forever near.

Hannah Gallant (16)
Chesham High School, Chesham

Crab Vs Porpoise

Crab versus porpoise, who will win?
One fights with claw, the other with fin.
Crab unleashes crazy ninja attacks,
Then stuffs porpoise's pieces into little sacks.
Porpoise reforms and grows 200 foot in height,
Like the monster in a Power Ranger fight.
Crab sees this and sheds a single tear,
Of course this is not due to fear,
But because he now gets to use the giant robot,
That he wanted since an egg in the cot.
Unleashing flaming flippers of doom,
Some may say the end for crab does loom.
Due to porpoise's relentless barrage,
Crab has no time to charge,
Luckily for crab he just installed new wings,
Guns, swords and pointy things!
The two giant gladiators in eternal stalemate,
Fighting forever, that is their fate!

Alex Tatton-Brown (17)
Chesham High School, Chesham

Presents For God

Just as some trees stand without leaves,
Beside them stand evergreens - ever-leaved.
Even when the sun has disappeared,
It leaves behind a beautiful peach light shining,
A brilliant luminescence staining every cloud with a silver lining.
An amazing sunset which no photo nor painting could do justice,
But the warmth of its memory heating our hearts, gleaming for just us.

Still smiling in the fading light,
As day melts softly into night.
The last blades of sunlight slice silhouettes on the horizon,
Blank, dark shapes awaiting detail from another sun rising.

People come and go, but lifetimes never end,
Even when boxed as presents for God, ready to send.
Lifetimes will remain remembered, whether short or long.
The sunbeams of life forever shine strong.

Not only a great man, but a hero in our eyes,
May he forever here lie in God's eternal sunrise.

Christopher Vincent (17)
Chesham High School, Chesham

The Mysteries Of Life

Life is unpredictable,
In every single way,
You can never tell what is going to happen,
In life from day to day.

But here and there odd things happen,
In life that make you ponder,
Sometimes mysteries do not get explained,
They make you think, they make you wonder.

Everything in life has a purpose,
From an ant to a bumblebee and trout,
But what do you think is the source of it all?
Nobody knows, we may never find out.

This is my poem,
This is my rhyme,
Life has many secrets,
Untold about time.

Charlie Vale (11)
Chesham High School, Chesham

Guilt

Guilt is a travelling beast.
It sounds like a shadow in darkened moonlight.
Guilt is a disease that riddles your paranoia.
It looks like an animal ready to pounce.
Guilt is a trader who sells cracked goods.
It tastes like a sour grape with an aftertaste.
Guilt is a room of memories you can't escape.
It smells like a pear which rots down suddenly.
Guilt is in your mind and you can't destroy it.

Jonnie Bayfield (12)
Cliff Park High School, Gorleston

Me!

I am a bear
Big, cuddly, warm
There for you

I am a vault
You have to get over me
To reach the finish line

I am a pencil
I get things right
I get things wrong

I am sand
Catch me
I fall through your fingers

I am a hair bobble
I stretch
I wrap myself around you

I am a pencil case
Put good things in
Take some bad out

I am wrapping paper
Sellotape and a present
Full of happiness.

Sarah-Louise Gee (13)
Cliff Park High School, Gorleston

Happiness

Happiness is all the colours of the rainbow
It sounds like joyful laughter
Happiness tastes like chocolate cake
It smells like freshly cut grass
Happiness feels like a silk robe
It is the sand between your toes.

Sophie Dye (13)
Cliff Park High School, Gorleston

Sadness

Sadness is creamy white,
The sound of rain on a hot summer's night.
Sadness tastes like warm milk,
It feels like bed sheets made of smooth silk.
Sadness smells like a dying flower,
It's like getting caught in an ice-cold shower.

Alex Durrant (13)
Cliff Park High School, Gorleston

Joy!

Joy is a warm, pink, summer's day.
It sounds like birds singing.
Joy tastes like freshly baked bread.
It smells like a daffodil.
Joy feels like a great big hug.
It is like lovely chocolate cake.

Holly Riches (12)
Cliff Park High School, Gorleston

Joy

Joy is baby-pink.
It sounds like children playing.
Joy tastes like chocolate cake.
It smells like the fresh air of spring.
Joy feels like sand running through your fingers.
It is a newborn baby!

Chloé Ellis (13)
Cliff Park High School, Gorleston

The Old Man

The old man is a slow snail,
He moves like a tired tortoise,
His skin is like that of a premature baby,
He walks like a withered cat,
He speaks like a croaky toad,
He shuffles down the street like an injured soldier,
Every step harder than the last.

Vicky Barber (13)
Cliff Park High School, Gorleston

Aeroplane

The aeroplane is an angry lion,
It moves like it's chasing prey,
It roars at take-off,
It is the most powerful thing on Earth,
It purrs along in the clouds,
In its environment, it's king.

Harry Yusuff (12)
Cliff Park High School, Gorleston

Love

Love is a twinkling star
It sounds like the birds in the sky
Love tastes like pink ice cream
It feels like bubbles in the air
Love smells like a yellow flower
It's like the whole world is a heart.

Claire Tye (12)
Cliff Park High School, Gorleston

The Burglar Is A Cat

The burglar is a cat,
He moves like a coin running across the table.
His fur is as sleek and soft as a silky blanket,
He sounds like a brand new engine purring, smoothly moving,
His eyes are big and glow like a nightlight in the dark,
The burglar is as light-footed as a mouse.

Robyn Disbury (13)
Cliff Park High School, Gorleston

Joy

Joy is a loveheart red,
It sounds like people having fun,
Joy tastes like fresh fudge cake,
It smells like shiny petrol,
Joy feels like a soft quilt,
It is a lush, colourful sofa.

Kieran Deeks (13)
Cliff Park High School, Gorleston

Fear

Fear is like a blackened sky
It sounds like the howling of a werewolf
Fear tastes like eating maggots from an apple
It smells like a man's dead body
Fear feels like dinosaur's scaly skin
It is as cold as the Atlantic sea.

Pierce Browne (12)
Cliff Park High School, Gorleston

Rage Is . . .

Rage is a fiery red
It smells of thick smoke
Rage tastes like hot chilli peppers
It feels like a bed of nails
Rage sounds like a volcanic explosion
It is a desert wasteland where the sand is too hot to stand on.

Ben Akerman (12)
Cliff Park High School, Gorleston

Kindness

Kindness is a pastel pink
It smells like red roses
Kindness tastes like juicy strawberries
It feels like a big hug
Kindness sounds like soft waves crashing against the rocks
It is a nice, big smile.

Stephanie Willimott (13)
Cliff Park High School, Gorleston

Anger

Anger is a bloody red,
It smells of stinky socks,
Anger tastes like out of date cheese,
It feels like rough carpet,
Anger sounds like people punching a brick wall,
It is a big, red ball around you.

Samuel Malley (12)
Cliff Park High School, Gorleston

Untitled

I can't see out the window
But I can see the sky
People running, screaming
It looks like it's going to rain
I see black, then white dots
And then a black line
I hear thunder and see lightning in my head
I don't want to go outside
And I don't want it to snow
I might get hit by flying snowballs
It's very quiet in here . . .
Anger rushes into my system
Anger makes you scream inside
Makes you go as red as blood
Makes you think of things you hate
Forces you to get revenge
It promises to come back again
And when it comes, it won't pass by
Until someone apologises
And then it walks off waiting
Until the next time.

Samantha Storey (13)
Cliff Park High School, Gorleston

Rage Is . . .

Rage is devil-red
It smells like rotten eggs
Rage tastes like gone-off milk
It feels like a rough rock
Rage sounds like crashing thunder
It is a big black volcano erupting.

Joe Jones (12)
Cliff Park High School, Gorleston

Me!

I'm very shy, shy as can be.
When Miss asks a question, I hope it isn't to me.

At home I'm quite lazy,
But yet very crazy.

My favourite animals are of course cats
And the most disgusting things are rats.

I have the best family ever,
We enjoy spending quality time together.

I love learning new things at school,
I think it is rather cool.

When I get older I want to live a great life
And make someone happy by being a decent wife.

I am one of these people who will help you through thick and thin,
I love to make unhappy people smile or even grin.

I'm a difficult person to be,
The best thing is, no one can be me, but me!

Jade Traves (13)
Cliff Park High School, Gorleston

Madness

Madness is a raging fire.
It smells of mouldy cheese.
Madness tastes of gherkins and custard.
Madness feels like a prickly hedgehog.
Madness sounds like a bridge is exploding.
Madness is like the planet Mars' surface.

David Moore (13)
Cliff Park High School, Gorleston

America

America,
America,
America.

What do you think when people say America?

Well, I think life, city life, under city life
Then here's the explanation, in America there's
Lots of things, money, people and life.
In the down-under bits of America
(The bits you don't see on television)
There's still life like the bums that live
Down amongst the garbage
And rats and dead things, there's life
The old man who never had a wife
Fought in the war and still survived
But what was the point of surviving?
What did they come back to?
No money, no one cared because all their family died
And no one knew they were even there
So they're a bit lost really, so all they do all day
Is sit in the garbage and hope, pray
Someone will care about them again
Someday they will die and no one will know.

Mary Waters (12)
Cliff Park High School, Gorleston

Happiness

Happiness is sunshine yellow
It smells of big red, roses
Happiness tastes of brown chocolate
It feels like a silk pillow
Happiness sounds like birds singing
It's a beach on a tropical island.

Lucinda Murray (12)
Cliff Park High School, Gorleston

I Passed Away

I died,
Like the leaves on a winter tree,
But the difference is . . .
Never coming home again.

I died,
I only feel coldness,
Nothing more,

Not . . .

Love of another,
Not the breeze of the wind going through my hair,
But as I say, I am never coming home again.

I died,
But here comes the day,
When all my family and friends come to say goodbye
And the last words I will ever treasure are,
I love you Daughter,
But I will always still be around.

Shannon Carr (12)
Cliff Park High School, Gorleston

The Weed

Robbers of the soil,
Dull, thin and scrawny,
Intruders with a crafty mind,
Talk and scheme about coiling,
Overruling ugly pests,
Dull and annoying.

Scavenging shade from other plants,
Between cracks they rise and rise
And strangle all life around them,
Without a care for who they hurt,
But one day they'll get tangled and dragged
And feel the pain they once imposed.

Daniel Coates (12)
Cliff Park High School, Gorleston

Snow!

Snow glistens in the light,
A blanket of snow, what a beautiful sight.
Crunch, crunch, crunch beneath our feet,
Stays in the cold, melts in the heat.
We stay off school and have snowball fights,
Wrapping up warm, so we don't get frostbite.
We build our snowman with his scarf and hat,
Looking so lonely, fancy that!
Me and my friends have a sled race,
I fell off mine and landed on my face!
The snow was so soft, it didn't hurt,
I'm so glad I didn't wear my skirt!
I have had a brilliant day,
I want it to snow tomorrow, I want it to snow every day!

Christie Richards (12)
Cliff Park High School, Gorleston

The White Stuff

When the white snow falls, everything glistens,
When the children come out, the snow listens.
Snowmen are all around, frosty and cold
And standing up tall like soldiers so bold.
It sparkles like diamonds in the sunlight,
It's a soft, fluffy carpet that glows bright.
The snow crackles loudly under our feet,
It melts so slowly when the sunrays beat.
Flutters like feathers falling from the sky,
Kids watch desperately hoping it will lie.
Snowballs fly furiously through the air,
Children laugh happily without a care.
Wanting a snow day from school the next day,
Praying the snow will never go away!

Emily Basey (12)
Cliff Park High School, Gorleston

Snow Poem

The snow is falling from the sky tonight,
Like a blanket, I watched by the firelight.
I sat and saw it glisten, past the moon,
To know I would be playing in it soon.
To build a big snowman in the morning,
It would be cold when the day was dawning.
I'd go outside in my soft woolly hat,
Come in and leave my wellies on the mat.
To throw snowballs at the people who'll play
And wish that I can go outside today.
Whether I am in or whether I'm out,
I always like to laugh, play and shout.
In the morning I crunch through the snow,
It will soon melt away, and it will go.

Sophia Nicholson (12)
Cliff Park High School, Gorleston

Everyone's The Same!

Everybody looks different,
Nobody looks the same!
Some people are tall, some people are short,
Some people are rich, some people are poor!
But inside, *everyone* is the same,
Nobody's heart is in their feet
And nobody's veins are yellow!

So why do people expect others to be like them
And why do people think they are better?

Everyone's the same inside,
No matter what they look like.

Gemma Harlow (12)
Cliff Park High School, Gorleston

Death

Death can be happy,
It can also be sad,
Loneliness can be caused by death.
At funerals, people cry,
Sometimes they cry happy tears,
Because the person they love has gone to a better place,
When someone dies, they are always with you,
In your mind, in your soul, in your heart.

Death can be hard to accept,
It causes anger and depression,
Immaturity and sleepless nights.
It emotionally mixes people up.
People sit around all day, lonely in a room,
Not knowing what to do.
Thinking about death,
But what they don't realise, they are always with you,
In your mind, in your soul, in your heart.

Finola Young (13)
Cliff Park High School, Gorleston

Creepy Weed

Slowly walking up the garden fence,
Quietly creeping like a robber,

Coiling round everything that gets in the way,
Weaving in and out of the fodder.

Its appearance is scrawny, green and thin,
Too much of it is overwhelming.

It pops its ugly head out,
Year in, year out.

An unwanted, depressing intruder,
That makes us want to shout!

Faye Humphrey (13)
Cliff Park High School, Gorleston

The Overtaking Emotion

Every day on the way to school
You are picked on
Not allowed to tell anybody
Scared in case they might attack you
You accidentally say something
And they're there, waiting for you

Every day from that point on
They beat you up
Laughing at you because you can't do anything
Then, the next day, you fight back
Pounding, kicking and crying
You try to stop
But your emotions take over
And yet . . . you enjoy it

For once you feel like you've beaten them, but . . .
They just stand there, watching you and laughing at you . . .
Then, all of a sudden, it's *the overtaking emotion and you* . . .

Kyle Watt (12)
Cliff Park High School, Gorleston

Me

I am confident but shy
Hate is the part I try to keep inside
My obsession is annoying
My memory should be better
I try to be friendly
My friends think I am loud
I feel unreliable
The pressure gets to me
But that's just *me!*

Alex Wilkinson (12)
Cliff Park High School, Gorleston

Snow Poem

Thickly-laid snow blankets the ground,
Freezing, icy chills that make you shiver.
Keep warm with a coat of winter woollies.
Snowflakes falling on the ground, icy cold.
When it gets warmer, it all turns to slush.
Everyone gets a cold and starts to cough.
Kids listen to the radio and wish,
To hear the school closures while getting dressed.
Snowball fights in the playground with their friends.
Icy pavements so you fall over, ouch!
It's so quiet, everyone is inside.
The snow listens to your conversations,
When you stand on the snow, it makes a crunch,
Snow is as soft as a fluffy blanket.

Sarah Harvey (12)
Cliff Park High School, Gorleston

Fire

Fire is a dragon that destroys
Anything in its sight,
It has no meaning,
All it does is burn and create heat.

It needs oxygen to breathe and to grow,
It can burn and tear through forests
As fast as a cheetah that is chasing its prey.

Its raging heat dances in the moonlight,
Like people drunk on a stage,
Showing off at anything.

Fire is the Devil hurting anyone and anything,
Pain is its game
And no one likes it,
Fire is anger.

Peter Townshend (12)
Cliff Park High School, Gorleston

Untitled

I remember it like it was yesterday,
He seemed to suddenly fade away.

I was only small and I was young,
I barely even knew him.
All I knew was that he was mine,
He was there for me,
Whenever I was sad and upset,
When it felt like I had no one left in the world.

He used to have so much fun with me,
When we played out in the garden
And we cuddled.

I love him so much,
But now he has gone.
Somewhere I cannot see him anymore,
I often wonder if he can see me
And if he's sitting beside me.
It feels like he is always with me,
It feels as if he has never left me,
Is he here or is he not?
I guess that I will never know.

I love him loads
And I always will,
I love him,
I love him,
I love you, Grandad.

Holly Tyler (12)
Cliff Park High School, Gorleston

This Is Why I'm Hurting

When I was only 18 months old,
he was taken away from me.
Now I have unanswered questions,
that no one can answer.
This is why I'm hurting.

He was like something perfect,
with no cracks or damage.
I always looked up to him,
every day.
This is why I'm hurting.

The problem is, I'm not complete,
there will always be a piece missing.
The piece is him,
but he's gone.
This is why I'm hurting.

There are lots of doors in my life
that are always shut.
This is where I can remember him,
I'm talking about my dad
and this is why I'm hurting.

Julia Prettyman (13)
Cliff Park High School, Gorleston

Padstow Harbour
(Inspired by 'Aud Laddeus Leaning Against Damson Trees' by Frank Kendon)

. . . And the sun rising over the still, cool sea.
And the lazy fishermen bathing in the sun,
Waiting for the first catch of the day.
And the ice cream men, setting up their stands.
And the first group of tourists wandering into the magical harbour.
And the children eating their melting ice creams,
Watching the enchantment of the boat's reflection on the still water.
And the paranoid parents' faces as children creep towards
The edge to look at the colourful fish below in the clear water.
And the kind boat owner talking to the passers-by,
As they listen intently like small schoolchildren.
And the local crab fishers, young but so determined
As their faces light up with joy when a crab is caught,
With the young apprentices watching, watching.
And the hungry people crowding round the pasty shop, mouths open,
Arms flapping like baby birds in their nest.
And the boats harbouring up after a long day out at sea.
And the tourists are wandering back to their cars,
Looking back at the harbour as they leave.
And the sun setting over the still, cool sea.

Keziah Henley (13)
Gamlingay Village College, Gamlingay

Song For The World
(Inspired by a visit from poet Richard Burns)

Go song to the lonely and oppressed.
Go song to those who grieve.
Do not be discouraged,
Do not let the world put you down,
Be sure that you never take the path of evil,
Resist, most of all, the ones who will lead you astray.
Fight against wrong and bad feelings that may live inside you,
Take with you a light that will shine in the darkest places,
Carry along with you a sword of peace to help those in need
And give the world a message in your never-ending melody.
Go song and free the world from the darkness that haunts it,
Go like a dove and let your beauty radiate on the ground,
Go like a waterfall, with power and might to change the world.

Jordan Macrow (12)
Gamlingay Village College, Gamlingay

The English Weather

The English weather changes all the time
From snow to wind,
Sleet to hailstone,
Sun to rain.

From shorts to woolly jumpers,
Sandals to bulky boots,
Flipflops to shoes,
Depending on the weather, you have to choose.

Suntan to fake tan,
Umbrella to canopy,
Whatever the weather, it goes on
Forever and ever.

Jamie Taylor (12)
Kingsbrook School, Deanshanger

My Seasons Poem

Wrapped up warm,
Landscape of brown,
Hallowe'en frights,
Gleaming orange pumpkins,
Trees with precious few leaves,
Misty mornings, fading light,
Autumn.

Woolly hats and scarves,
Snow blanket,
Christmas cake,
White wonderland,
Trees bare,
Smiling snowman,
Winter.

Hats come off,
Hopeful shoots promise more,
Easter Bunny's coming,
Pale green frail leaves,
Buds are growing,
Longer days,
Spring.

Shorts and T-shirts,
Sunglasses and suncream,
Holiday laughter,
Red, blue and purple flowers,
Richly coloured trees,
Kids playing,
Summer.

Daniel Lefevre (12)
Kingsbrook School, Deanshanger

Summers Of Passion
(Inspired by 'Magic Box' by Kit Wright)

I will put in my box . . .
The sweet scent of lilies and roses,
The gleaming of overpowering gems,
The soft, icy blanket of snow.

I will put in my box . . .
The love and care from the deepest of people's hearts,
The tingle when you put chocolate to your lips,
The peace and tranquillity which lies beneath the earth.

My box is fashioned with . . .
Transparent, precious stones, rubies, sapphires and amethysts,
Which shimmer and glisten in the illuminate ray of sunlight.

I shall remember my box as . . .
'The summers of passion',
So delicate yet blooming with colour and beauty.

Lucy Thorpe (12)
Kingsbrook School, Deanshanger

The Library!

Sitting in the library,
Reading a book,
I'm filled with enjoyment,
One smile from Mrs Sharpling,
That's all it took!

Others are sitting,
Doing their work,
But some are gossiping,
With a smirk!

Awais A Saeed (11)
Kingsbrook School, Deanshanger

Why Is There Racism In The World?

I'm watching the match,
The star who's black, like me, touches the ball,
They start to scream,
I'm saying to myself, *what's wrong with them all?*
This is supposed to be a game of fun and entertainment,
Not mocking and disbelief,
My team, Man Utd, won,
But also racism from the crowd won,
I live in hope and fear,
That racism will soon become clear,
It shouldn't be in today's sport,
Or anywhere else like school or court,
Get out racism, we don't want you here,
Love and compassion is what we hold dear,
You'd better be listening,
Because I've tried to make myself clear.

Adrian Alara (12)
Kingsbrook School, Deanshanger

Snowflakes Falling

Snowflakes falling all around,
Gently settling upon the ground.
Children playing and having fun,
Building snowmen with everyone.

Making snow angels in the frost,
Snowballs being thrown and tossed,
The sun's going down in the sky,
The snow has stopped and said goodbye.

Annie Thompson (12)
Kingsbrook School, Deanshanger

Why?

Why is their water dirty?
Why are they dying?
Why are there orphans?
Why?

What did they do wrong?
What was their sin?
What did they forget?
Why?

Why are they so poor?
Why do the children die?
Why is there not enough food?
Why?

Is it the country?
Is it the heat?
Is it because they've done something wrong?
Why?

How can we help them?
How do we stop this?
How can we give?
We can give to charity.

Lizzie Millidge (12)
Kingsbrook School, Deanshanger

Flowers

They dance with the wind,
Their scent sweeter than fruit,
Their colours shine like the rainbow,
Their stems as straight as soldiers.
Flowers brighten people's hearts,
Just like they brighten mine.

Sarah Belmont-Colwell (11)
Kingsbrook School, Deanshanger

The Life Story

T ime is nine months till birth,
H e is born giving his parents pride,
E verybody has heard.

L ittle do they know,
I t will not turn out
F ine as planned,
E van Korburrow kidnapped.

S eventy thousand pound ransom,
T wo months to pay.
O ut of money, but desperate, it is managed.
R aldough the kidnapper is untrustworthy,
Y oung death for Evan.

Max Ikin (13)
Kingsbrook School, Deanshanger

Comic Relief

We all know it's about
The big red nose,
Fun and games
And funny shows.

But this year it's all
About your hair,
So gel it up
And spray it red.

Aside from the fun,
What's it really all about?
I'll tell you,
It's all about the people in Africa,
The ones that need your help.

Rebecca Basketfield (11)
Kingsbrook School, Deanshanger

The Death Of The Stuffed Cat

She saw a solitary, shiny jar
And her hands reached out,
She wanted a biscuit,
So round and so yummy,
Some food that would definitely
Fill up her tummy,
The cloud, the biscuits,
A cloud full of rain,
All bottled up.

A living room so small,
Squashed between four walls,
A creamy blur,
A roaring purr,
Not a hiss, definitely not a shriek,
Her eyes so wide, not a peek.

A rip, a tear,
Which is not rare,
A creamy white tail,
There no more.

Taylor Willbond (13)
Kingsbrook School, Deanshanger

Food!

Food, food, so nice!
I could probably eat anything twice,
Delicious food on my plate,
Dangling around like some fish bait,
People looking at your food,
Don't you find it rather rude?
When you're full, right to the top,
You feel like you're gonna pop!

Mitchell Brown (12)
Kingsbrook School, Deanshanger

Memories

Still a shock to remember
Falling, falling off a horsebox's back,
Plunging to the ground, shell-shocked,
Times when only you feel the pain,
Not knowing, what was to happen.

Still a joy to remember,
Diving, without the water hitting you.
Sliding silently through the wet blue pool,
Touching, bouncing, surfacing,
A magical dream come true.

Still a shock to remember,
The adrenaline running through my body,
I was shaking in my shoes,
My heart skipped a beat,
Where was I? . . . I was lost!

Still a joy to remember,
Seeing her face light up as she was racing towards me,
I jumped for joy as I realised who it was,
Nothing could stop her now.

Still a shock to remember,
The love of a lost one, gone!
Night and day, day and night,
She was not there,
Where was she?
She had gone.

Clare Booth (12)
Kingsbrook School, Deanshanger

Death

Her long cape blows, as red as blood,
Her eyes like golden fire,
She brings a chill on summer days,
Her face gives off golden rays,
Her hair is wavy and stiff like wire.

Felicia Gatenby (13)
Kingsbrook School, Deanshanger

My Love Poem

You came into my life like a candle in the wind
Blowing your loving to everyone but me it seemed
I couldn't believe my luck that day when you turned and winked
You smiled at me
I smiled at you
Our eyes locked in an eternal sleep
For evermore our love shall not part us nor
Shall we part it
Together we stand forever.

Ollie Bishop (12)
Kingsbrook School, Deanshanger

Inside His Head

(Inspired by the screenplay 'You Made Me')

A Pandora's box,
Already been opened.

A tub of laughter and happiness,
Tightly sealed down.

Soiled trousers,
A lonely laughing stock.

A partly-frayed rope,
Swinging, strands snapping.

A dark black hole,
Sucking away all love.

A roughly cut diamond,
Multi faceted.

Pushed and pulled,
Who wants me?

Rebecca Houseago (12)
Kingsbrook School, Deanshanger

Seasons

As the children ride their bikes,
Daffodils start to appear.
The sound of the birds singing in the trees,
Sends a tickle down my spine.
As the sun beams down on us,
All the flowers open up with joy.

As the children scream with laughter,
As they splash each other in the pool.
The smoky smell of sausages sizzling on the BBQ,
The smell of fresh cut grass in the air,
As the whirring lawnmowers set to work.

When the children play in the brown crispy leaves,
Lots of screams and shouts come from the woods,
As the leaves blow around in the breeze,
The branches sway back and forth,
Drinks are spilt and food is dropped when families enjoy picnics.

As the snow floats down,
It brings smiles to people's faces.
The coldness of the snow when children play snow fights
Sends a tickle down my back.
The softness of the white, cold, soft snow
Is like a big, puffy, soft pillow.

Chloé Moore (11)
Kingsbrook School, Deanshanger

Inside The Head Of A Boy From A Torn-Apart Family

(Inspired by the screenplay 'You Made Me')

His parents in separate rooms,
An endless slide into nothing,
In the corner, aliens fighting men in suits,
A sealed box full of memories.

And nothing to fall back on.

Kieran Price (12)
Kingsbrook School, Deanshanger

Monday

Monday morning feeling low,
Back to school I've got to go,
I pull the duvet over my head,
Please, please let me stay in bed,
No time for that, there's lots to do,
Get washed and dressed, I've lost a shoe,
Books all packed in my bag,
It's Monday morning, what a drag!
Down for breakfast, tea and toast,
Then the postman brings the post,
A knock at the door, it's my mate,
I hope that the bus isn't late,
Just enough time, my homework to finish,
First period maths, then English and Spanish,
At lunchtime it's basketball practise for me,
Followed by science and ICT,
At last the bell rings, it's time to go,
Mondays always seem to go slow,
Although looking back it wasn't that bad,
But when I get home I'll feel really glad.

Daniel Coll (12)
Kingsbrook School, Deanshanger

In My Head!

A box full of laughter and fun,
Only to be opened when sad,
A padlocked room with the past in,
An open room with the future.

A tape of happy times on the shelf,
A tape of bad times in the bin.
A wardrobe full of dance kit,
To be opened when I'm a star.

My nan not being alive or near,
But in my heart she lives.

Danni Harris (12)
Kingsbrook School, Deanshanger

Beth, The Bear

Beth, the bear is always there
Deep down in the forest of the Rockies
Where the sun shines high in the Canadian sky
During the long summer months
She fishes in the streams for the salmon
That swim beneath the crystal clear waters
When she's finished feeding
She takes a nap
And then hears a snap
Like the biggest snap ever
Then comes a poacher, trying to find something to kill
He spots Beth
She fears for her life and dives into the thick, thick grass
Where she is safe and can't get spotted
As the months go past, the leaves fall onto the grass
As wintertime approaches
The sky turns grey as the snow begins to settle
Beth gets ready to hibernate from the cold winter snow
Until spring returns again.

Thomas Taylor (12)
Kingsbrook School, Deanshanger

Mystical Creature

It surveys the darkest skies,
Swaying through with its golden eyes.
Glistening in the shadows of caverns beneath,
It has wings as light as a feather,
It's the only thing breaking up night and day.

There is no underestimating its vision,
Whilst it glides over mountain edges and past rivers.
From the bright sunrise to the moon's face,
This creature is one of a kind.

Joe Smith (12)
Kingsbrook School, Deanshanger

Jasper

Going, going, gone . . . there goes Jasper faster than a bullet!
With his long pink tongue flapping, galloping like a racehorse
His black velvety fur shining in the sun
His flappy ears forced backwards by the wind
Running through fields of grass cutting them like a razor's edge

His big brown puppy eyes beckon for the toast on the table
Licking his lips every second
Each lick sends a long string of saliva to the kitchen floor
As we carry the leftovers to his bowl, he spins around with glee
He scoffs down the food in a millisecond or two

As he returns to his bed after a long walk
He slumps down on his bed and turns his eyes backwards
As he sleeps he has dreams of running in the field once more
His legs are 'sleep running' and he barks at nothing

He gets next-door's cats in his sights
Like a leopard in disguise he gets ready to pounce
He lets out a warning bark from the bottom of his stomach
Jasper runs as fast as he can looking as vicious as a grizzly bear
But despite his efforts the cats are way too fast for him
Rejected by the cats he gives up and gives it a rest for the day

Jasper is the best dog in the world, I'll never let him go
Even though he can't catch cats, I still love him so!

Sam Clarke (11)
Kingsbrook School, Deanshanger

Chocolate

Chocolate is yummy
In my tummy
Different shapes and sizes
Sometimes you get them as prizes
Lots of different flavours
Have it for lunch with Quavers
But it won't do you any favours!

Ross Lloyd (12)
Kingsbrook School, Deanshanger

Pillow Fight

I once had a pillow fight,
I almost hit the ceiling light.
I hit my brother on the head
And fell off of my mother's bed.

I once had a pillow fight,
It lasted almost half the night.
I hit my sister round the face,
So she ran off at quite a pace.

She ran off and told my mum,
So she smacked us both on the bum,
But I was only three,
So you can't blame me!

Gemma Pullen (12)
Kingsbrook School, Deanshanger

Weather

Weather is clever,
Weather is strange,
You never know when
It will change,
Sometimes it's hot,
Then sometimes it's not.

Each day is different,
They're never the same,
So why should we
Ever complain of the rain?

We're never happy,
We always moan,
Whatever the weather,
Be it hot or cold!

Miles Luckett (12)
Kingsbrook School, Deanshanger

A Week In A Student's Life!

On Monday we don't like the day
Because the sun's always hidden away.

On Tuesday we have PE,
Oh my goodness, I've hurt my knee.

Wednesdays don't get any better,
On this day we have Mr Messeter.

Thursday is a good day,
We have science and we get to play.

On Friday we get to go home
And then we can play on our mobile phones.

Saturday is the *best!*
Cos we get a called-for rest!

On Sunday my homework's all in a pile,
But hey! I get to watch my favourite programme, smile!

Emma Norman (13)
Kingsbrook School, Deanshanger

What Can I Hear In The Park?

What can I hear in the park?
Children playing happily.
What can I hear in the park?
Birds squawking as they fly right past.
What can I hear in the park?
The sound of laughter, the sound of joy.
What can I hear in the park?
Water flowing down the river.
What can I hear in the park?
Goal!
What can I hear in the park?
Nothing, it's getting dark!

Peter Rhodes (11)
Kingsbrook School, Deanshanger

The Island Dream!

There the island is,
The golden beach of dreams is staring at me,
The wind waves the trees like a stampede of elephants,
We arrive on shore,
As I get off the boat I can feel the sand through my toes,
I look back at the sea, it looks so clear and blue,
From a distance the beach looked so small,
But now it seems so big,
I lay my bag down, take my T-shirt off,
And tiptoe into the sea,
The waves are getting bigger by the minute,
I decide to swim further out to sea,
I feel something snip my foot,
I start to panic,
I look down but it's only some seaweed,
I carry on swimming,
My feet no longer touch the floor,
I get scared so I swim back to the beach,
I lay down on my towel
And doze off,
Next thing I know I am awake in my bed,
It was all a dream!

Nathaniel Nero (11)
Kingsbrook School, Deanshanger

Football Poem

The ball at your feet,
Wait for the whistle,
The ref blows and everything starts,
You pass the ball back into your defence,
Kick over the top and into a good position,
Your teammate plays it through,
You score the goal,
You win the cup,
Everything is wild.

Matthew Dimmock (12)
Kingsbrook School, Deanshanger

A Unicorn At Heart

By this magical waterfall
The unicorn stands proud and tall
Shimmering, the waterfall glistens in the moonlight
Oh, what a stunning sight
With a gleam in her eye
Her sight makes you sigh
A shake of her mane
To show she's not tame
She glides over the water
The air breaks before her
She lands with style
You can almost see her smile
Water droplets dive from the air
They land in her gorgeous hair
What a picture
Of an amazing creature!

Helen Worrall (13)
Kingsbrook School, Deanshanger

Days Of The Week

On Monday morning the sun shone down,
All over the busy people in town.

On Tuesday morning the sun did boil,
It even dried out my brand new soil!

On Wednesday more bursts of hotter sun,
The kids played out and had such fun.

On Thursday cold winds blew,
But the sky was clear all day through.

Friday's sun was the hottest we'd had,
It made us all extremely mad!

Luke Gibbard (12)
Kingsbrook School, Deanshanger

Roberta Starr And Her Motor Car!

Roberta Starr,
Roberta Starr,
Lost control in her new motor car.

Round and round the street she races,
Not even going
In slow paces.

Roberta Starr,
Roberta Starr,
The fastest ever motor car.

Ever seen,
Ever seen,
The nicest, leanest steam machine!

Round she slips,
Round she slips,
Just before some fish and chips.

So exciting,
So exciting
And has just the greatest inside lighting!

Motor car,
Motor car,
With the weirdest owner, Roberta Starr!

Roberta Starr,
Roberta Starr,
The worst motor driver by far!

Victoria Roberts (12)
Kingsbrook School, Deanshanger

A Poem Of Anger

You feel it bubble from your toes,
Going up, up, up.
It's shooting through your legs now,
Like a fierce tiger running to its destiny.
Gathering speed as it heads for your tummy,
You feel slightly queasy inside.
It won't stop now,
Getting ready for the big moment.
It's sliding and slithering up your throat,
A red snake about to lunge
And then it releases on its prey.
You shout it out of your lungs,
A fiery volcano that's been set off.
You're screaming now,
Your blood getting thicker by the second.
A satisfying feeling it is to shout
At a person that drove you too far.

Katie Arkle (13)
Kingsbrook School, Deanshanger

A Week Of Summer Weather

On Monday my skin was pale,
So I will tell you the sun's tale.

On Tuesday the sun was bright,
All through the day and night.

On Wednesday I could feel the heat,
I got a tan on my feet.

On Thursday it was cool,
So I jumped into the pool.

On Friday's cloudless sky
Got me on a sunbed to lie.

On Saturday I can't remember,
So on Sunday I met up with Amber.

Francesca Boyle (13)
Kingsbrook School, Deanshanger

Anger

Anger turns day to night
And sun to rain,
It can cause a fight
And lots of pain.

When anger turns to rage,
Your body becomes tense,
Your feelings are let out of their cage,
The hatred you can sense.

Anger burns you like a fire,
Your enemy is trembling with all their fears,
Your blood has turned to wire,
There are voices in your ears.

The redness of your face,
Lets everyone know you're going to shout,
Your enemy wants to leave this place,
But is trapped and can't get out!

Anger bursts its enormous head,
That was the poisonous punch,
It's time to put anger back in its bed,
The time has passed causing the final crunch!

Amber Fox (12)
Kingsbrook School, Deanshanger

Friend Or Foe?

As the anger takes over me,
My head starts to fill with blood,
I turn red.
I feel like another person is taking over my soul,
I have no control and lash out,
I lay on the bed crying.
I feel so disappointed in myself,
The anger disappears out of my system,
I am me again.
I know soon he will be back though.

Leah Gay (13)
Kingsbrook School, Deanshanger

Alone

I'm lost in a world of sorrow,
I'm buried in a deathbed grave,
I can hear the owls hooting,
I can see the stars twinkling,
I can feel the draught hit my cheek
And I can sense fear in the wind.

I'm the one that stands out here,
Amongst these dreaming, daring fears.
The dark walls surround my skin,
I'm there, I know it, buried within,
I scream out loud; I face my fears,
The echo of me carries on going until
The last screech dies.

'I'm alive!' I shout. 'I'm here!' I cry,
But the words don't come out,
They're locked up, sound asleep,
All alone without me.

Rachael Urquhart (12)
Kingsbrook School, Deanshanger

Feelings

Butterflies, dizziness,
Faintness,
Must be love.

Heart throb, legs wobble,
Head spins,
Must be love.

Dry mouth, eye twitch,
Faint smile,
Must be love.

Head spins, feet move,
Heart stops,
Must be love.

Elisha Cowley (13)
Kingsbrook School, Deanshanger

Alan's Head

In Alan's head is a box full of laughter,
But it's closed and locked tightly inside
With a padlock that has no keyhole,
Behind a slide where he had fun.

In Alan's head is a picture of embarrassment
From when he wet himself,
He wishes for a spaceship going into space,
It lands on an unknown planet.

In Alan's head he has a miserable time,
All he sees is his mother shouting,
Inside it all, lays a teddy bear,
That he got when he was a baby.

Elliott Nichols (13)
Kingsbrook School, Deanshanger

Anger

Your blood is boiling,
You have lost your temper,
Your hands are now fists,
You want to break out.

Your jaws are clenching,
Your eyes are red,
You're ready to pounce
And you have no control.

You have lost control,
Your body's taken over,
You are no longer you,
You're someone else.

You need to relax,
But you cannot,
Because you are being controlled by
Anger!

Robbie McBreen (13)
Kingsbrook School, Deanshanger

Life And Death In The Trenches
(Inspired by 'Suicide In The Trenches' by Siegfried Sassoon)

I saw an ordinary soldier lad
His wounds were bloody and bad
Laid on the filthy mud to rest
While the soldiers were put to the life and death test

I was waiting to go over the top of the trench
The gas made the lads wrench
Angry men were covered in mud and rain
To discover the filth and cruel angry pain

The noisy crowds were roaring with delight
When the soldiers got on the ships to go and fight
The bands stopped playing and people just walked away
Then the soldier turned around and everyone had gone astray.

Matt Taylor (18)
Lonsdale School, Stevenage

In The Trenches
(Inspired by 'Suicide In The Trenches' by Siegfried Sassoon)

I knew an uneducated soldier lad
He smiled at life when times were bad
Could sleep through noises in the night
But wide awake was he in the morning light

In cold trenches tired and alone
So hungry, he was just skin and bone
He shot himself in the head
Never mentioned again, nothing said

When I think of those cheering crowds
If they knew, would they be so proud?
Sending their boys out onto the killing field
There, one by one, being killed.

Martin Brassett (18)
Lonsdale School, Stevenage

The Difference Between Life And Death In The Trenches
(Inspired by 'Suicide In The Trenches' by Siegfried Sassoon)

I knew an uneducated soldier lad,
who had not washed, so he smelt bad.
His clothes were damp, he looked like a tramp.
His face was covered in dirt and muck
because he had forgotten to duck.
The air around was full of death,
he could taste it with every breath.

Jo Brimson (16)
Lonsdale School, Stevenage

Valentine

Not a red rose or a satin heart.

I give you a snake.
This is long and it lasts for many years,
Just like our love.
Long and sinewy,
It will twist and turn through our years together,
Holding us fast in its tightening jaws
And embracing us forever.

Here, take it,
Love it and care for it,
It's dangerous and poisonous,
Just like our love.
We shall respect it and not mistreat it.

I'm trying to be truthful.

Not a cute card or kissogram.

I give you a snake.

Its shed skin will shrink to a wedding ring if you like.

Kai Dunn (13)
Lothingland Middle School, Lowestoft

Valentine

Not a cute puppy or a diamond ring.

I give you a river.
It is a glittering necklace polished with oil.
It promises life through mountains and valleys.

Here.
It will suffocate winding through your mind,
Like a snake.
It will grow wider and deeper.
Until it begins to part.

I am trying to be truthful.

Not a rose or some chocolates.

I give you a river.
Its cold touch will drop off your fingers.
Fast and slow,
The velocity will take you.

Take it.
Its eddies will drown you in a whirlpool of love.
So very hard to resist,
One sip will pollute your blood.
The fever will take control.
But when will it stop?

Jasmine Marsh (12)
Lothingland Middle School, Lowestoft

Haikus

Dark forest of trees,
Leaves rustling. Be aware,
The path is leading.

The grey rough gravel,
Crunching as the footsteps pass,
Leaving prints behind.

Chloe Shields & Mia Taylor (12)
Lothingland Middle School, Lowestoft

Ode To My Bed

O! You wondrous bed,
You exquisite bed of mine,
You are everything to me,
Your soft squeezy mattress envelops me,
The exquisite design of your base I worship,
I applaud the times you welcome me,
I quiver at the sight of your 'Silent Night' label,
You are everything to me,
I relax on you beneath the stars,
You nourish my dreams as I hide deep into you,
Into those winter mornings,
Snuggling in your deep softness,
I savour you on those early mornings,
Reluctant to leave your side,
You're like an angel from above,
You're divine and comfortable,
My bed,
My one and only bed.

Adam Glover (13)
Lothingland Middle School, Lowestoft

I Want To Fly

I want to fly:
Through the clouds of cotton wool.
Through the sapphire raindrops.
I want to fly up through the sky,
As high as I can go.

I want to fly.
Into a land that only I can reach.
Where it snows through night and day,
But always has the heat of May.

Thomas Broderick (12)
Lothingland Middle School, Lowestoft

Valentine

Not a red rose or a satin heart.

I give you a ring.
The shine is like our happiness
As it used to be.
It has been worn for several years
And the shine is fading, just like our love.

Here.
It will remind you of me,
Broken-hearted.
It will make you think
How much we loved each other.

I am trying to be honest.

Not a box of chocolates or a kiss.

I give you a ring,
Its diamonds will blind you.
Faith and honesty
Is here
And will always be here.

Take it.
Its shine will turn to rust,
If you like.
Fierce.
Its shine will blind your eyes
And will stay with you for as long as you live.

Vicky Howard (13)
Lothingland Middle School, Lowestoft

Valentine

Not a red rose or a satin heart.

I give you an orange.
Its bright colour is the light of our relationship.
As it is peeled,
Our true colours shine through.

Here.
Break off each segment,
Our love falls apart.
The sour juice will sting your lips,
Like a fierce kiss from a lover.

I'm trying to be truthful.

Not a fluffy teddy or chocolate.

I give you an orange.
Its skin will stay under your nails.
The scent will stain your fingers
For as long as we are together.

Take it.
Throw the peel of the orange away,
As you peel it
You may foresee the future,
Of our love and happiness.

Michelle McClean (13)
Lothingland Middle School, Lowestoft

My Room

My door slows as it drags along the carpet floor.
In the room is my dark silver CD player.
The neon blue audio meter clicks as it hits the glass stopper.
The smoke from my many incenses fill the room,
Choking whoever doesn't appreciate it,
Smothering them with a white mist of apple odour.
I lie down on the sea-blue bed.
The many glass bottles on my desk.
My mum tries to rid me of them, again and again,
Always failing.

Cameron Gallagher (13)
Lothingland Middle School, Lowestoft

Valentine

Not a red rose or a satin heart.
I give you a ring,
It is a star wrapped in a box.
It promises light and brightness,
Like our love.
Here.
It will blind you like the sun,
Like our love.
It will make us one.
We will possess each other
And we will drown,
In our love.
With this ring . . .

Sherri Sawyer (13)
Lothingland Middle School, Lowestoft

Valentine

Not a red rose or a satin heart,
I give you a sports car.
It promises engine roar,
Showing the excitement of our love.
Its exhaust perfume will tempt you to its door.
The sweet nectar-smelling leather seats will envelop your body.
Its vibrant metallic shine will sparkle like our love.
This prancing black horse is as priceless
As any of your fine bracelets.
Its two red stripes passing over the bonnet are like us,
Always parallel, never parting.

James Brabben (12)
Lothingland Middle School, Lowestoft

Odd Ode

O' fantastic cat of mine,
Most wonderful of all.
When you are indoors, you lay on the chair,
Because you are a lovely lazy thing.
Your brilliant stripes,
Make me smile with delight.
My house would be empty
Without you, my cat.
Never shall I abandon you out in the cold.
Never shall I leave you without food.
Never shall another cat lie on your chair,
Without you, my cat, my life would not be complete.

Victoria Drysdale (13)
Lothingland Middle School, Lowestoft

Hospital Room

I dashed down the dull and gloomy corridor as fast as I could,
But when I got to the door, I wasn't so sure that I wanted to open it.

It was a stiff door handle,
I opened it with precaution
Because I wasn't sure what to expect.

The room was bright,
Mainly because the corridor was dull.
I saw a shiny metal bed
With some machines close by.

My little brother was standing next to me.
He was worried because he couldn't see over the bed.
I was only tall enough to see my mum's face.

My dad's eyes were gleaming with joy,
My mum was laying down in the bed,
With my sister in her arms.

Jordan Kingsley (12)
Lothingland Middle School, Lowestoft

Chickens!

Oh, my clucking chickens,
Pecking away,
All day, every day.
They're like little rockers,
Head banging all the time,
In my garden.
They are made for me,
All four queens of the house.
They are called,
Mitch, Bushie,
Speck, Saver,
Heroines of our home.

Thomas Thorogood (12)
Lothingland Middle School, Lowestoft

The Scream

I stood on the craggy wooden bridge,
My heart was full of emotion.

I watched the bridge narrowing into the distance,
My eyes were swollen with tears.

I listened to the sound of death swirling through my mind,
My tears were running down my skull-shaped face.

I saw the river of drab colours rolling beneath me in a rage,
My body was dressed in black mourning clothes.

I was touched as people from everywhere patched up the washed-up strip of land,
My legs wanted to take me down to help them.

I watched the swirls in the sky, the river and the land,
My heart was full of emotions.

Emma Walton (11)
Lovat Middle School, Newport Pagnell

Yep, That's Me

Yep, that's me, crying my eyes out
Behind the veil
Because I'm a black person
My fat lips tightly shut
Not nice

Yep, that's me
With long plaits and tears running down my cheeks
Then onto my shoulders
Not nice

Yep, that's me
All on my own
With no one else to comfort me
Not nice.

Greg Pape (11)
Lovat Middle School, Newport Pagnell

My English Rose

My English rose,
When will I see you again?
When will I smell your sweet scent?
When will I feel your soft skin?
Do not fear my sweet rose,
For I shall be back soon.
Although it's dark and dreary,
I am still fine, I still live.
I still love you.
My memory of you is true,
As I know that you are waiting,
Waiting for me.
The sky is only grey because I miss you.
Never worry my sweet rose,
I will return to you and Jimmy.
To love you once again.
How is Jimmy?
Does he cry?
Tell my boy I'm alright.
Tell him I still love him,
As I still love you.
Tell him that I'll hold him,
Just like I used to do.
Darling rose, do not cry.
Please my darling, wipe your eyes.
Dry your tears,
Dry his too
And I'll come back,
Come home to you.

Lily Morris (12)
Lovat Middle School, Newport Pagnell

Torture

Where am I?
My head is spinning like the grenade through the air
My heart is thudding like the gunshots all around us
I'm so confused

What has happened?
I'm deserted, all alone
But now I'm surrounded
By people deep in sleep
But will they ever wake up?
I don't know

Why did they do this to us?
They gassed us like cowards
So now I feel like I
Have let my country down

When will I return back home again?
To see my family once more
Will I get back home for Christmas
Or will this pain never end?
Am I in Heaven, Hell
Or have I survived this torture?

Emily Anderson (11) & Kathryn Myers (12)
Lovat Middle School, Newport Pagnell

Think!

Think of the children on the street
Think!
They have hardly anything to eat
Lying there in piles of rags
All they have is a few plastic bags
Staring at the children all around
Having to sleep on the ground
People don't care to see
But what would you do if it was me?

Beth Lloyd-Jones (12)
Lovat Middle School, Newport Pagnell

Beneath The Willow

Beneath the willow
Buried down deep
Baby rabbits fast asleep

Beneath the willow
As quiet as a mouse
A tiny insect is building his house

Beneath the willow
Growing tall
Ivy's climbing up the stone wall

Beneath the willow
Humans dressed in brown
They're there to chop the willow down.

Charlie Ball (12)
Lovat Middle School, Newport Pagnell

My War Hero

Where are you?
When will you be back?
How long will it take?
Will you ever be back?
Why haven't you written?
Are you injured or dead?
When will I see you?
Do you remember the last words I said?
You haven't been gassed have you?
Is that why you can't return to me?
Please say it's not that bad
It just can't be
Please come back
My war hero.

Chloe Cartwright (11)
Lovat Middle School, Newport Pagnell

Thoughts About Life

T roubles and tears
H appiness and joy
O bvious feelings to girl and boy
U nhappy or sad
G rateful or glad
H idden thoughts that are forever locked up
T hese are feelings from the heart
S omeone special is always there, don't forget that they really care

A moment in life
B e true to yourself
O n days when you're down
U nmistakeable love and friendship is always shown
T ruth and lies will always remain within your lives

L ove and joy
I nterests and thoughts
F riendship and feelings
E very day you are reminded of these wonderful things.

Grace Finnigan (12)
Lovat Middle School, Newport Pagnell

Tsunami

T is for tsunami's terrible wave,
S is for staring at the devastation it's left behind,
U is for understanding the situation of others,
N is for naming the people who have died,
A is for the awful destruction the tsunami has caused,
M is for making small steps without looking back,
I is for incredible stories people have to tell.

Charlotte Heggie (11)
Lovat Middle School, Newport Pagnell

On The Racetrack

I hear the crowd cheering as I walk out onto the track
As I walk by people, I feel them pat my back
I see the other racers getting into place
I realise where I am and my heart begins to race
So much depends on this short run
Everyone is nervous, everyone is glum
The gunshot rings out and off we go
Those who are left behind are too slow
We race towards the first bend
I know that I will soon reach the end
The finish line is in sight
The cameras are flashing bright
I'm so close to running through the ribbon
But my hopes are suddenly hidden
Another runner races by me
Faster than a wave from the sea
They're going to get there first
Suddenly I get a burst
Of speed and I catch up
I really am pushing my luck
It's just between him and me
I'm running so fast I can hardly see
I look sideways and see him
But will I be able to win?

Ben O'Donnell (11)
Lovat Middle School, Newport Pagnell

The Summer

S is for the sun that comes and warms the planet
U is for the umbrellas that have been put away
M is for making sandcastles under the sun in the sand
M is for the massive picnics we all enjoy
E is for everything special in the world
R is for red of the fire in the sun that warms us all up.

Stephanie Lynes (11)
Lovat Middle School, Newport Pagnell

Tiger

The swift determined tiger proud of himself.
With orange fur, not realising how dangerous.
Can't stop marching, too observant,
Aware of what's going to happen
Always thinking two steps ahead
Claws so sharp, able to pierce skin
Can pounce at any time, so just stay alert.

Matthew Sandall (12)
Lovat Middle School, Newport Pagnell

Tsunami Poem

T error rushing down your street
S urrendering your life under the wave
U nhappy relatives crying at your death
N o hope of living
A nimals swim next to you in the street
M ums and dads sobbing over your lifeless body
I nto the wave your lifeless body is dragged.

Paul James (12)
Lovat Middle School, Newport Pagnell

The Tsunami

The tsunami might come.
The tsunami might hit.
The tsunami might knock you off your feet.
The tsunami might destroy your life.
The tsunami might sink your house.
The tsunami might hurt your friends.
The tsunami might crush your country,
But the tsunami can't steal your hopes.

Milan Odedra (12)
Lovat Middle School, Newport Pagnell

I'm Sorry

Dear Mum and Dad,
I'm sorry for who I am,
I'm sorry, I'm sorry, I'm sorry,
I can see I make you worry,
You know I would change if I could,
You know I would even though I told myself it wasn't my fault,
Every nightfall and every morning rise,
I feel like wolves are calling for me,
As they bash me from side to side,
On the way home from school
A group of boys always manage to get me
And take me into a bush and do things you couldn't imagine
And I feel dirty afterwards so I take a shower
When I get home from school
When you're at work
I scream your name all the way through
Mum, I know I shouldn't be telling you this
For all the pain I have put you through
But now I've reached the end of my tether
And I can't go back, I've snapped
I'm sorry for who I am
But now they might feel bad for what they've done
And I'll never see you again
So I'm sorry for who I am and what I've done.

Tara Smith (12)
Lovat Middle School, Newport Pagnell

Tsunami

T oo much danger about
S o much death lurks
U nderwater, no one can get away
N ear the ocean is death
A huge wave comes out of nowhere
M y friends have died
I live alone.

Ryan Massey (12)
Lovat Middle School, Newport Pagnell

Pleading

I came out of the theatre
It was dark
A gang of drug dealers followed my every footstep
As I ran down the alley
I tripped
They cornered me at the dead end
I pleaded for mercy
They said nothing as the moonlight shone on their faces
I tried to climb the wall
I got to the top
I fell
I didn't know why
I saw the jagged knife in my leg
I heard a gunshot, did it hit me?

David Gaskell & Jack Overton (11)
Lovat Middle School, Newport Pagnell

Prowling Tiger

Prowling tiger so big and proud
Beautiful glowing orange fleece
Immense paws strolling the ground
Visitors gape at the razor-sharp teeth
Waiting patiently for his afternoon snack
Wonder what it will be today, chicken, beef, pork?
His sneaky hideaway
Here it comes, his afternoon snack!
Tearing away at the fleshy bones
Munch
Munch
Munch!
Fast asleep . . . *zzz* . . .

Sophie Treslove (12)
Lovat Middle School, Newport Pagnell

Unpleasant Bullies

A is for the anger in their faces.
B is for beating, bruises all over.
C is for the consequence of seeing them on my way home.
D is for the dirt that they throw in my face.
E is for encouraging, his friends cheer him on.
F is for fate, they decide what mine will be.
G is for gang, they huddle around me.
H is for harassment, maybe I should report it to the police?
I is for injuries, I have to hide them from my mum.
J is for joking, laughing as I suffer.
K is for kicking, is violence really necessary?
L is for loser and other horrible names they call me.
M is for massive, they're bigger, stronger and older than me.
N is for noises, I try to scream.
O is for offence, is what they're doing illegal?
P is for panic, my heart thuds.
Q is for quiver, every time they're near.
R is for rags, that's what they call my clothes.
S is for scars, not only on my body, but in my mind too.
T is for tease, they wind me up.
U is for unpleasant, I hate it when they're around.
V is for verbal, the abuse goes on and on.
W is for why? What have I done to deserve it?
X is for excuse, they can't justify themselves.
Z is for Zoe, my new best friend, after I told someone I was being bullied.

Lynsey Dorn (12)
Lovat Middle School, Newport Pagnell

Tiger

He patrols his land like a worried policeman
His beady brown eyes checking around
Food tonight he thinks to himself
As he moves along the muddy ground
He gives everyone that 'stay away' look
All this while keeping his pack under control.

William Wimmer (11)
Lovat Middle School, Newport Pagnell

Do Not Judge Me By My Face

Do not judge me by my face
Nor my colour, size or race.

You don't know what goes on inside
When you make your comments sharp and snide.

I know you've written me off with a tick or cross,
I'll just put it down as not my, but your loss.

I've got so much more beneath my skin,
If you just asked I'd let you in.

But you think you have got me sussed,
As someone lesser to you I trust.

Maybe next time you could wait
And get to know each personality trait.

Other people you can attract
But I don't like the way you act.

The way you think you know me to the core,
I suppose you've seen 'ones like me' before.

Do not judge me by my face,
Nor my colour, size or race.

Sarah Maunder (14)
Mayflower County High School, Billericay

Did You See Her?

Did you hear her crying
That child on the floor?
Did you see her face
Before you shut the door?

Did you give a second thought
To what you had just done?
Did you know she loved you more
Once you asked her to come?

Did you see her laugh
Giggle at her new name?
Did you see the perfect picture
Before you broke the frame?

Did you know her secret
The one she kept from you?
Did you know she loved you
And thought you loved her too?

Did you think it was right
To end her life as you did?
Did you somehow see the goodness
In hurting your child, a kid?

Did you want to harm her,
Hurt her, oh so bad?
Did you have to kill her?
She was all you had.

Did you think of what you'd done
After you did the deed
Or maybe you thought it was a relief
One less mouth to feed?

Melissa Newnham (13)
Mayflower County High School, Billericay

Thunder And Lightning

A hot, sticky night. You can't get to sleep.
A child somewhere plays with the skylights
And ghostly shapes of the room are monsters in the dark
1, 2, 3, 4 . . . a giant's tummy rumbles in the distance

I get up and tiptoe to the window
Then suddenly a flash pierces the black of the night
A shaft of jagged light like a sharp steel knife
1, 2 . . . a giant's tummy growls for food under my window

I hide under my sheets
A short circuiting socket comes for me through my sheets
1 . . . a giant's tummy growls for me at the bottom of my bed

The storm moves away
The air is fresher
I sleep like a cat 'til morning.

Kirsty Dyce (11)
Onslow St Audrey's School, Hatfield

Playing Football Is Like A Kettle

I am a shiny kettle, when playing on a football pitch
When someone really annoys me, it's like flicking on a switch
I get hotter and hotter until I start to glow
The person I'm marking then stamps on my toe
Now I'm really boiling and steam begins to appear
Everyone can see it coming out my ears
My manager calls me over and says, 'You listen to me!
If you don't calm down, you'll be off for a cup of tea!'

Sam Adamson (12)
Onslow St Audrey's School, Hatfield

Poems Are . . .

Poems are things that come from the heart,
Poems are a kind of written art.
Poems are the languages of the minds,
Poems are a text that is one of a kind.
Poems are songs with no music,
Poetry is enjoyable and people like to read it.
Language of a king, babble of a peasant,
It makes people feel all happy and pleasant.

Poems are the windows to the world,
There are lots for boys and lots for girls.
Poems are doors to the mind,
You have to open them to see what's behind.
Poems speak the language of the soul,
Use your brain to take control.
I used to think poems were boring,
Then I opened my mind and I did some exploring.
Now I think poetry is great
And so do a bunch of kids in Year 8!

Brian Ratliff (12)
Onslow St Audrey's School, Hatfield

Fire

The fire has glowing eyes
Embers dance
Crackles like creaking bones
Red, orange and yellow
Warm, golden hair
Throw in the wood
While it burns and sparks
All is left is ash.

Laura Charalambous (11)
Onslow St Audrey's School, Hatfield

Omens

The omens they are coming,
Coming swift as a bird of prey with eyes that rival the dark of the night
Coming dark as the dark itself with teeth that rival that of the great lion
Coming silent as a feather dropping on the loamy soil with
                                            fingers that rival ice
Coming evil as Hades in the pits of Hell with hearts to rival
                                            the colour black
The omens they are killing
Killing with laughter as shrill as a banshee with claws to rival
                                            that of Cerberus
Killing with delight to match that of a child licking an ice cream
                                            on a hot summer's day
Killing like they are pure death . . .
The omens they are leaving
Leaving, but not without consequences, with smiles to rival that of God
Looking down on the wonder of His world
Leaving the scene of the crime like madmen from sanity with
                                            corruption to match that of the Devil
Leaving to return another day, another tragic day . . .

John Neicho (11)
Onslow St Audrey's School, Hatfield

The Wind

I can get through a doorway without being seen
And be everywhere yet not be seen.

I can be destructive and shake tall towers,
But I can blow through the garden and not wake the flowers.

When I'm angry, my power is violent,
But when I'm calm, I'm totally silent.

Robert Walton (11)
Onslow St Audrey's School, Hatfield

Sonnet

Yourr hair's so fine, it glistens in the night,
I want you to be mine, I love your so,
Your tender touch is smooth, so holds me tight,
My love for you is fast and never slow,
I give you all my love, so just be mine,
Her bright blue eyes are like the deep blue sea,
O, girl why do you have to be so fine?
I'll climb the highest mountain just for thee,
When I see you, I want to serenade,
You will always be my only true love,
Your everlasting beauty will not fade,
To me you are a blossoming young dove,
What else can I say? You're one of a kind
And all the day you are upon my mind.

Seamus Kerwick & David Chandler (12)
Onslow St Audrey's School, Hatfield

Office Equipment

The fax machine,
Sticks out a long tongue,
As the message arrives.

The computer screen,
Blinks one large eye,
Like a cyclops.

The keyboard buttons,
Go click-click,
Like chattering teeth.

Adam Kyprianou (11)
Onslow St Audrey's School, Hatfield

Tomorrow - Haikus

The colourful bird
Sings on the branch of a tree
Calls for a new day

The sun fades away
Another day passes by
Wait for tomorrow.

Sara Ismail-Sutton (11)
Onslow St Audrey's School, Hatfield

Spooked

It's a normal winter's night,
The rain's pouring and the thunder's crashing,
Lightning thrashing, waves are splashing,
Light all around, everything in sight.

The wind is like a wolf, howling through the cracks,
Running through the woods, lapping at the water,
Wolf cubs howling, badgers growling 'cause it's been slaughtered,
The wolf is tired, he's gone back to the pack.

The tree's waving in the wind,
Outside the window, tapping on the glass,
Swaying like fingers, reaching down to the grass,
The lightning struck the tree and it was singed.

In the morning, the sun rose,
We were glad to see the sun again.

Adam Evans (12)
Raunds Manor School & Sports College, Wellingborough

Sunset At Sea

Fishermen setting off,
Hopefully for a good catch.
The sun hiding behind thick clouds,
Peeping out now and then,
Making for a gloomy evening
And then, the sea got rougher,
Like a young child, waiting for dinner.

Then, the storm started,
Thunder!
Lightning!
The sea tossing and turning,
This way and that
And then,
Nothing . . .

George Firth
Raunds Manor School & Sports College, Wellingborough

Guilt

As I sat in my cell
I just couldn't put out the hell
Of the guilt burning inside

It tears away your confidence
It pulls you on your knees
Then I start to cry
And I start to think why

I didn't mean to do it
It happened on its own
But when I saw him lying dead
I knew what I had done

So as I sat inside my cell
I could not put out the hell
Of my guilt still burning inside.

Joseph Pickering (12)
Raunds Manor School & Sports College, Wellingborough

Squirrel's Seasons

The sea is calm
The clouds are bright
The palm trees glow
Everything's good in the sunlight

Hay barrels roll
A nice summer's breeze
People paying their tolls
To get out of the blistering sun

Autumn's here
So now I fear
To go shopping for food and stash it near
Then down to the pub for a pint of beer

Winter is now
So take a bow
You've lasted all year
Stay inside, don't go out
For a blizzard is here.

James Hennessy (12)
Raunds Manor School & Sports College, Wellingborough

Fears

My eyes are watering lots of tears,
As I run from my fears.
Their long, thin legs stretched out wide,
But I still run and try to hide.
Where I'll hide, I do not know,
I only hope that they will go.
Somewhere far away from me,
But I wish I knew where that could be.
They come closer, I start to shriek,
They see me in the corner and I shout, 'Eeek!'

Clare Cowling (12)
Raunds Manor School & Sports College, Wellingborough

School

The bell rings, we trail in.
We sit down and answer our names.
The teacher tells us it's not fun and games.
We go to lessons first, second, third,
Then the fourth comes, *maths*, that's absurd!
Numbers and page, books open and close,
We are just about ready for a doze.
Dining hall calls, food queues a size,
Sausages, burgers and meat pies.
Listen to the children shout and cry,
The bell rings, hear the children sigh.
Another two lessons come our way,
But after that it's home time, hip hip hooray!

Lewis Chinnick (12)
Raunds Manor School & Sports College, Wellingborough

Love Jigsaw

A jigsaw is made
A couple is made
They fit together
Like a bird and a feather
They link arm in arm
Palm to palm
They are a puzzle
No one can undo
No one can separate
They're stuck fast like glue
They make up a core
They are a jigsaw.

Alex McLean (11)
Raunds Manor School & Sports College, Wellingborough

It's Christmas Today

Waking up on Christmas Day
With lots and lots of things to say
All my presents 'neath the tree
Waiting there for the family

I'm so excited, I just can't wait
It's Christmas Day, I can't be late
All those presents wrapped up neat
Then I'll have something to eat

The dinner always is the same
My mum's cooking is not a game
The hot stuffed turkey looks really nice
With potatoes and veggies, then mince pies

My excitement grows as the day goes by
Clouds are drifting in the sky
Full of glistening fluffy white snow
To make our hearts and fingers glow

As I go to sleep tonight
The moon and stars are shining bright
Let's tuck ourselves in our beds
For us to have sweet dreams in our heads.

Imogen Davis (11)
Raunds Manor School & Sports College, Wellingborough

Storm At Sea

It was a soft blowy wind,
When all of a sudden a dark storm came across us,
Then a really strong buzz,
I think it was lightning,
A loud bang, the lightning was insane,
The sky was clearly in pain,
No shelters around!
And lightning ready to pound.

Oliver Buckley (12)
Raunds Manor School & Sports College, Wellingborough

Fish!

Under the deep blue sea
Fishes are swimming around
They look so beautiful
So calm, so colourful

Fish, coral, rocks
So wonderful to see
Oh how I want to be down there
Swimming with the fish in the sea

So light and bright
It's so lovely to see
All quiet
No sharks

So, so peaceful
All so kind
Everything gets along
It's just so peaceful.

Ellis Snow (12)
Raunds Manor School & Sports College, Wellingborough

Love With My Family

I was mad with myself,
Using my foe to cry on.
I was mad with my brother,
I told my foe to calm me down.

I was jealous with my brother,
Mum and Dad acting like I was not here.
I think I thought I was invisible,
But, my foe helped me out.

Now I know I am still here,
I know Mum and Dad *still* love me!

Charlotte Simmons (12)
Raunds Manor School & Sports College, Wellingborough

Pea-Green Boat

There with blue skies in the clear lake they sit,
In their little wooden pea-green boat.
Two women think it's funnier to sail than knit,
Always they wonder if they will stay afloat.

The beautiful bright yellow sun shone down,
Sending shadows of their dresses onto the water.
They are always happy for they never frown,
The two young ladies, a mother and daughter.

All the autumn leaves of green and brown,
Sway in the distance far, far away,
Soon the leaves are all sure to fall down,
As it gets dark at the end of the day.

The youngest one says, 'Mother may we come again?'
'Of course we can my dear Lorraine.'

Natalie Johnson (12)
St Alban's Catholic High School, Ipswich

India

A mother trying to teach her young calf
A little leopard joyful at its first kill
An elephant clumsily treads its path
A lion stalking its prey lies deadly still
Travellers forever coming and going
The market noise and wonderful smells
Snake charmers on their flutes are blowing
Lots of people crowding round the wells
In India many sights meet your eyes
But nothing compares to the sunset
Over the horizon the beams they lie
Not a more magical sight have you met
I can sit for hours just watching the light
Enjoying the hours when day turns to night.

Bethan Sidoli (12)
St Alban's Catholic High School, Ipswich

Natural Love

Gibbons are the acrobats of the wild
Moving on nature's nimble tightropes
To heart's desire, like a toy to a child
But how does the gibbon with love cope?
As he gets up and sings with great volume
To attract the love of his life
The female gibbon seems to assume
That his singing is bound to cause trouble and strife
The female gibbon's mate is against her follower
And great trouble-filled war breaks out
And as they fight for great love o'er her
The one with the greatest love will win, no doubt
Over love, most precious they did fight
Now both their souls are in the clouds through the night.

Sam Richards (13)
St Alban's Catholic High School, Ipswich

Louisiana In May!

The flowers and trees swaying in the breeze,
Bundles of pink joy basking in the sun,
Pendulous catkins swinging with such ease,
Sun shining brightly like a yellow bun.

The winding path invites you to explore,
The white needle towers out of the ground,
The giant willow tree who all adore,
Standing proud dominating all around.

Short lime-green hedges in neat and tidy rows,
An ocean of bluer than blue sky,
See a speck of soft, fluffy clouds like bows,
A hint of a building as you pass by.

Shut your eyes on a dark November day
And fly to Louisiana in May.

Ruth Pope (13)
St Alban's Catholic High School, Ipswich

The Bridge

The sun is rising on the bridge of steel,
Everyone is busy beginning the day,
Carefree and happy that's how I feel,
The tourist boats pass and here's what they say,
'As you look up the Bridge of Steel you'll see,'
People take pictures of the wondrous sight,
The birds soar above them as carefree as can be,
I think the bridge looks even more gorgeous at night,
I walk along the pathway as if in a dream,
The lorries drive over the marvellous bridge,
The sun is high now and makes the water gleam,
I feel like I'm on the edge of a ridge,
More boats have come now, all sailing along,
By this time tonight, they all will be gone.

Louise Duffy (13)
St Alban's Catholic High School, Ipswich

Florida Sunset Sonnet

What's so good about Florida sunset?
I like the silhouettes of the people
As I like the way the colours are set
I like the way the ocean's waves ripple
I wish I were there on the darkened pier
Beneath the sunset, so wide in its breath
You say to your friends, 'I wish you were here'
And you'd love the way the picture has depth
I like the orange that fades into pink
With the purple that fades into a blue
The aquamarine sea that seems to wink
And shimmers like the early morning dew
The ripples, the colours, the silhouettes
That is what makes a Florida sunset.

Rachel Mulvey (12) & Jess Simpson (13)
St Alban's Catholic High School, Ipswich

Myself

My hair sits loosely upon my shoulders
My face, worn down from the strain of the world
I sit, slumped in a lonely chair
Others around me just sit and glare

Like a delicate fruit
My layers of calming peacefulness are peeled away
Making me feel bare
I block out all around me, totally unaware

I feel like a worn-out sun
Not wanting to shine anymore
Good expectations cloud my mind
A spare minute just to think, I can never find.

Katharine Etheridge (14)
St Alban's Catholic High School, Ipswich

I Feel Like A Shadow Of Myself

I feel like a shadow of myself,
Hiding from light,
Hiding from truth,
Hiding from fear.

I feel like an outsider,
I feel far away,
Like the moon,
Cold, pale and hard to reach,

Hard to touch,
Like a thorny black rose,
With an other-world, cold beauty
But rooted to the ground.

I feel like a sea of salty tears,
Unable to let the water leave my eyes,
I grew up too quickly,
I suppressed the little girl inside.

Jennifer McCarthy (14)
St Alban's Catholic High School, Ipswich

That Bully

That bully was coming after me again
So I needed a place to hide
I saw the school door was open
So I quickly ran inside

He was lurking round the corridor
Calling out my name
He said I should come out and fight like a man
Not to play this silly game

He said he was getting closer
My heart was beating fast
I thought he was going to kill me
And I'd be part of the past

There he was walking closer and closer
He punched me to the floor
And as soon as he was about to leave
The teacher walked through the door.

Leonie Guiler (12)
St Alban's Catholic High School, Ipswich

Snow!

The snow is falling
The flakes are white and glowing
The ground is white
My hands have frostbite

Everyone wears hats and gloves
People get pushed and shoved
People sleighing all around me
I feel like a hot cup of tea

Days off school
That's really cool
February weather
All the better.

Natasha Crawley (12)
St Alban's Catholic High School, Ipswich

The Invalid
(Dedicated to children with severe disabilities at Heathside School, Ipswich)

I am the disabled one you talked of,
Watchful eyes - scornful, critical, without thought, without love.
Your eyes screamed a piercing 'abnormal'.
Reminded me who I was,

Discarded me as nothing for I was nothing.
Chance passed me by.
I looked nor acted like you,
But what I felt was overpowering . . .
You were my allies - I *hated* you,
You reminded me who I was,

You lived my life to its full,
You *stole* my life.

Soil surrounded me with love,
Drowned me in warmness,
Put the meaning of compassion back into hugs,
Held my hand as I returned to the dust,
See and believe what you took from me . . .
Remember . . .

Yet the tight blanket released its hold.
Set me free, let me live.
And as I rise, tears fall, as I recall . . .
I am who I am, who I am.

Polly Jackson (15)
St Alban's Catholic High School, Ipswich

Who Am I?

Who am I?
Am I the star that guided the wise men
Or am I the stream that washes clean the scars of the day
Or could I be the gentle wind that sweeps away all the debris of the past?
For when I look in the mirror, I don't see me
I see a never-ending rope reaching far into space.
I see a hill as high as the sky.
I see a stream giving life to the dead.
I see a cloud, sometimes I bring good news.
other times bad.
But if I were an animal I would see.
A turtle with powerful back legs that spray and kick back all distractions.
Other days I'm a hedgehog that holds all feelings
and homey touches inside
Then people ask me who I am, all I can say is;
I can be who I am, but I cannot display to others what I am.
For I can be a powerful storm billowing away at the restless sea.
Or I can be a blade of grass being whipped by a distraught wind.
As a friend I am a helping hand or a battering ram.
But whatever I do
I'm still me.

Katie Piper (12)
St Alban's Catholic High School, Ipswich

The Frosty Fluff

My heart is beating
Keeps on repeating.
I lean towards the window.

The freshly pressed shirt of sky
And the whiffing sound that comes by.
I open the rusty window.

The fluff that comes down on my nose,
Twitches and disappears quickly.
I start to shiver and put my scarlet jacket on.

The rich brown trees sway in the lively wind
And that wet smell is increasing.
I put my glossy black boots on and open the solid yellow door.

One after the other it's falling down gently,
Over on top of each other, layers and layers are rising.
I can hear the bushes whispering.

The white blank page of field,
Where children rush in to screaming,
I step into the deep icy crystals all piled up surrounding me.

I lean on a cold passionless wall,
Looking at the astonishing view,
I can hear the frosty icicles jingle and glisten.

It's flickering on the ground,
Not making a single sound.
I trample on the frozen path and scoop it up into my hands.

It tastes of air and smells of boiled water,
It shimmers of light and shines like a diamond.
Now I know what it is!
It's soft like a dewdrop on a delicate leaf . . . *snow!*

Srilekhini Kadari (12)
St Alban's Catholic High School, Ipswich

Cool

It annoys me 'cool'
Who invented the stupid rule?

In the nineties cool was
'Be a sheep, be a lemming'
Spider plants create clones
Must have: hoodies, Nike trainers and mobile phones

'We are cool
We bunk off school, get drunk, stoned, fail exams -
Join our group . . .
Gang
Crew
Who the hell are you?'
I am just me!

Now it is all
'Be different man, liberate your mind
Come along just for the ride!'
Now difference is cool
Still skive school, still get drunk and stoned, fail exams
There still is no change - the difference makes them all the same
A fashion they cannot see . . .
But I can and *I am still me!*

Fighting the pulls of teenage society.

Georgia Keogh-Horgan (16)
St Alban's Catholic High School, Ipswich

The Wings Of An Angel

Sometimes I wonder who I really am.
Am I a fox, really fast and sneaky
Or am I a cow who sits and eats all day in the field?
I sit here with my blondish-brown hair
And my blue eyes wondering what the meaning of my life is.
Sometimes I feel all alone; no one to share my tears with.
But other times I feel the world is comforting me.
On some days I want to scream and shout,
Other days I don't feel like going out.
I feel like a tiny knot lost in a long strand of hair.
Sometimes I wonder what I will become in the future.
Will I become a writer? Will I become a celebrity?
Sometimes I can't hide who I actually am,
Though I've tried and it hurts others.
I wonder when my reflection will show who I am inside.
But whoever I am or whoever I will be
I know I will always have the wings of an angel standing by me.

Shannon Veitch (12)
St Alban's Catholic High School, Ipswich

Inside A Soldier's Head

Inside a soldier's head
Are many sad and depressing memories.
There's a distinctive sound of gunfire and shots
And immobile bodies of friends they've lost.
Every night he lays awake,
Wondering if he'll make it home to support his family,
Or if he'll be there when they grow up or when they get married,
But when he sees the first glimpse of the sun in the morning,
He thanks God for him lasting another day
And he prays and prays, He'll let him last so he'll see his wife, May.

Jelani Blair (14)
Stantonbury Campus, Purbeck

Will You?

Will you hold my hand?
Will you walk with me?
Walk along by the sea wall,
Looking out to the sea,
Where the seagulls cry overhead,
Where the ships go past up or down the Thames.

Will you sit and hold my hand as the sun is setting?
Will you sit and hold my hand while we dream?
Will you sit with me on the settee?
Will you hold my hand while we are watching TV?
Will you give me a cuddle?
Will you love me?
Will you protect me from harm?
Will you always make me feel special?
Will you?

The answer is always, 'Not now, maybe tomorrow'
But those tomorrows are running out!

Samira Sadiq (12)
Stantonbury Campus, Purbeck

Snow

The forecast said that it would snow,
I went to bed hoping
That when I opened my eyes,
It would be here.

I got up in the morning,
Quickly opened up the curtains,
Rubbed the sleep out of my eyes
And heard my sister cheer.

White stuff lay on the ground,
But I had to go to school.
I got my bike from the shed,
It was very hard to steer!

Adam Billingham (13)
Stantonbury Campus, Purbeck

About My Originality

Born in London,
Originally from Bangladesh,
I am a Muslim
And I follow the Islamic way,
My home language is Bengali
And it's good to hear it said,
I go over there,
And there are six seasons in a year,
We were once part of Pakistan,
But then we hit 1971
And got our independence,
As a country of our own,
In the summer, it's really hot,
But in the winter
It's like the spring over here in England.

Atif Talukdar (14)
Stantonbury Campus, Purbeck

Inside A Soldier's Head

I cannot deny the fear in my eyes,
Nor the torment,
Confusion or sighs.

The stench of death
Is all around us,
Friends, flies and foe.
Underneath the ground we dig,
Building a temporary home.

The rest we have is so little,
Yet more precious
Than the weight of gold.
When daylight comes,
You know the angels are above,
Full of warmth for you to hold.

Natasha Davies (14)
Stantonbury Campus, Purbeck

Inside A Soldier's Head

Shells echo
Rifles stutter
Try to keep my discipline

Knees weak
Minds break
Try to keep my discipline

Men crumble
Lost lives
Try to keep my discipline

Orders in
Charge at dawn
Try to keep my discipline

Sunrise
Souls surrender
Can't keep my discipline.

Andrew Webb (14)
Stantonbury Campus, Purbeck

Inside A Soldier's Head

Inside a soldier's head . . .
There is pain and confusion,
His mind is scarred by the war.
There is hope and faith.
His mind is never at rest.
There is loss and fear.
He thinks of all the things
He misses and says,
'Maybe I can go tomorrow.'

Eavan McFall (14)
Stantonbury Campus, Purbeck

Fatherless

He's gone,
He didn't look back,
He didn't turn around . . .
I keep believing he cares,
He's gonna eventually turn around
And notice that he is wrong.
He makes promises
And I keep believing he didn't say them, it was just my imagination
Because he never keeps them.
I love him but I can't explain why I love him,
Except to say he's my birth father,
Even though he didn't look back to see if his daughter was okay,
He says sorry like it's an every-minute thing, it's a bunch of lies,
He's sorry and promises he won't do it again.
All I have to do is block it out
And act like it was my imagination,
Yet it hurts after a while . . .
Some fathers die so basically,
I'm fatherless.

With some guy that comes around,
Promising and saying he's sorry,
But if he says he's sorry then he wouldn't have to say sorry
Every time I talk to him
And his promises, they're nothing.
It's like I'm fatherless,
This man says he loves me and misses me
And I give and gave him so many chances,
But then he breaks it,
He doesn't look back
And notice I'm hurting, it's like he doesn't care . . .

Even though he says he loves me and cares,
Rubbish, sometimes I wish he would just stop calling altogether,
So I wouldn't have to hear his stuff;
His words, 'sorry,' 'promise,' those words they mean nothing to him
Nor me anymore, those words are useless, they have no meaning,
He's used them like some toilet that's in a public place
That everyone uses . . .
I'm fatherless.

Amy Myers (14)
Stantonbury Campus, Purbeck

Newcastle

Rain clouds high and concrete low
Summer sun and winter snow
A market place with stalls of meat
Kids with footballs on the street
Lads and lasses 'doon the toon'
The Hoppin's fair in breezy June
Newspaper stands in the town
Hardworking hands, tough and brown
Voices yelling in persuasion
In your face, verbal invasion
Accent lingers in the air
Cold, red faces stop and stare
Pubs and clubs open till dark
Football cheers from St James' Park
Strong brown ale that grandads sip
Geordie tongue and vice-like grip
Pocket knives up bad lads' sleeves
Outsiders labelled them as thieves
Tough old grannies with shopping trolleys
Buttoned coats and broken brollies
Mams with pushchairs in a bus queue
The Tyne's a reassuring view
For me to watch the water roam
Lets me know I'm back at home.

Catherine Whitmore (14)
Stantonbury Campus, Purbeck

Mask Or Me?

If you look at my mask
Whom shall you see?

A faded photo
Of the man I am to be?

The actions of a thought
Not yet conceived?

The silence of a word
Not yet believed?

The lies that are not seen
Become truer than confession

The wanting for nothingness
To become possession

If you look at my mask
Whom shall you see?

A photo? A thought? A word? A lie?
Whom shall you see?

Could there ever be such a thing as me?

Cameron Akitt (15)
Stantonbury Campus, Purbeck

Winter

A deadly season full of sorrow
Or a season full of beauty
Snow; a white sheet covering the sky
Rain clouds hover above our heads, ready to pounce

Snowball fights everywhere
The snow looks like dandruff in your hair
Fog limits your sight
Like the clouds blocking the moonlight
Winter.

Stuart Atkins (12)
Stantonbury Campus, Purbeck

Inside A Soldier's Head

I'm cold.
Water drips down my back.
It seeps into my bones
And soaks into the thick mud.
I'm scared,
The night is endless,
But not silent.
Explosions rattle around me,
Screams pierce the darkness.
A rat runs over my foot,
Scuttling into the darkness.
Lucky rat!
You can run away,
I cannot.
I stay at my post
And listen
And wait
And watch.
The relentless guns
Roar in the distance.
Out there, a faceless enemy
Also watches and waits.
Is he scared
Like me?
Dawn creeps up,
Lighting the mist that hovers
Over the trenches.
And now -
Silence.
My breath hangs in the icy air.
This is it.
My final effort.
The final push.
Over the top.
I am in a world
That has gone mad.

Richard Ackland (15)
Stantonbury Campus, Purbeck

Homework! Oh Homework!

Homework! Oh homework!
I hate you! You stink!
I wish I could wash you
Away in the sink,
If only a bomb
Would destroy you to bits.
Homework! Oh homework!
I hate you to bits.

I'd rather take baths
With a man-eating shark
Or wrestle a giant
Alone in the park,
Eat Brussels and liver,
Write 20 lines
Than tackle the homework
My teacher assigns!

Homework! Oh homework!
I hate you the most,
I wish I could send you
Away in the post,
I simply can't see
Why you even exist.
Homework! Oh homework!
You're last on my list!

Rachel Baker (13)
Stantonbury Campus, Purbeck

Mates

To pick you up
When you are down
Always good to have around
To make you laugh
To make you smile
Always makes your
Time worthwhile
To stick by you
A good true friend
There until
The bitter end
Always honest
Tell you how you look
They're definitely
In my good books!
They make me feel safe
And happy inside
You can be yourself
You don't have to hide
Return good favours
Look after your mates
That's what makes
A good friendship great!
And with loyalty, honesty
Love and trust
That's how a me
Becomes an us!

Heather Ross (13)
Stantonbury Campus, Purbeck

My Life

At the moment it's like a whirlpool,
Spinning round, taking everything in.
This everything is mates, boys, family and school,
Not to mention wanting to look thin!

That's my life.

Life as a teenager is a challenge of 5 years,
The ups and downs are in there.
Arguments, mood swings and tears,
Not to mention what to do with my hair!

That's my life.

So if ever I'm feeling down, not glowing,
I get told it's just a 'thing'.
For if I keep on going,
I can find out what tomorrow brings!

That's my life.

Alicia Perkins (13)
Stantonbury Campus, Purbeck

I Loved Him!

Why did it take him over?
Why couldn't it leave him be?
Why am I living all alone?
The cancer ruined both our lives,
It's not fair!

The last thing I said to him was,
'You can make it!'
But it should have been, 'I love you!'
What if he thought I did not love him?
It's not true, because
I loved him! So much!

Mari Edwards (15)
Stantonbury Campus, Purbeck

My Special Place!

My special place is as warm as a hot cross bun
There's plenty of space to run and have fun
It's nice just to sit by the pool and relax
Until someone jumps in and then you get splashed!

The smell of the fresh cut grass on the course
Is almost as nice as the smell of tomato sauce
When I'm there, I love to play football
But that's not as much fun as seeing your annoying sister
                                              fall in the pool!

My special place is the king of fried foods
It's where the king of rock and roll was born
So now you must have guessed where my special place is
Yep, that's right, it's America!

Jack Chalmers (12)
Stantonbury Campus, Purbeck

War

War is about fighting
Fighting for honour

War is about battle
Battling for your country

War is about death
Killing your enemy

War is about victory
Winning the battle

War is about memories
The memories in your head

War is about remembering
Remembering those who died

War tears us apart.

Ashley Maycock (13)
Stantonbury Campus, Purbeck

The Beach At Brene

There once was a beach at Brene,
But nobody's recently been,
There were shops all around, but they've fallen down
And now the sea's gone green!

There once was a beach at Brene,
But nobody's recently been,
There was a funfair, but there's nobody there
And now there's nothing to be seen!

There once was a beach at Brene,
But nobody's recently been,
'Cause people sat in their chairs, with the wind in their hair
And left it very unclean.

There once was a beach at Brene,
But nobody's recently been,
There was sand in the air and it went in their hair
And the things they shouted . . . obscene!

Jake Bloomfield (13)
Stantonbury Campus, Purbeck

My Special Poem

My special place is exciting and warm,
The birds and the butterflies come around in a swarm,
The sun is as warm as a fresh English fry-up,
But nothing is as refreshing as a handmade shake
In a cool stylish cup.

The feel of the water splashing in your face,
Is better than the taste of a new strawberry lace,
But the best thing of all is seeing your brother,
Getting pushed in the pool by your very own mother.

Paul Osborne (13)
Stantonbury Campus, Purbeck

My Special Place

A place where worries cannot come
A place where relaxing is all that's done
A place where you let loose and feel free
A place where there's nothing but sea
That's my special place!

A place where there are no cares
A place where the wind blows in your hair
That's my special place!

My special place is mine only
So make your own you old phoney

A place where worries cannot come
A place where relaxing is all that's done
A place where you let loose and feel free
A place where there's nothing but sea
That's my special place.

Verishua Maddix (12)
Stantonbury Campus, Purbeck

Special Place

S ecrets I can hold in here
P eople I can remember
E verything I love
C an be found in my special place
I can do what I want
A nd no one will see
L ife is so much easier when I'm left to be

P lacing myself on the bed
L aying comfortable
A nd reading
C an be so relaxing and
E verything bad goes away.

Annette Nunn (13)
Stantonbury Campus, Purbeck

My Special Place

Who needs a special place?
Who wants to be calm?
I prefer a smack in the face.
I prefer to do some harm!

Karate is where I like to be.
Karate chills me out.
Karate makes the best of me.
Karate calms my pout!

If I decide I want to kick 'em,
I'm sure to send them flying.
If I give 'em the eyes, I might as well flick 'em.
You'll still see them crying!

And if you want a piece of me,
Come on, I'm stood here waiting.
You really want to mess with me?
I'll use your head for baiting!

Do you think I'm a bully
And I want to see you cry?
Then you haven't met me fully,
Cos I'm as sweet as pie!

Katie Woodward (12)
Stantonbury Campus, Purbeck

Softly

Softly the children sit in rows
Softly the sand covers my toes
Softly the gravy hits my beef
Softly the caterpillar crawls on the leaf

Softly the spider spins its web
Softly the love comes in Feb
Soft is the butterfly in the willow
But softest of all is my pillow.

Adrian Edwards (12)
Stantonbury Campus, Purbeck

My Special Place

The swing swaying backwards and forwards just like the wavy sea.
The sun as hot as a cake just out of the oven.
The birds are as beautiful as a newborn baby.
The swings are as creaky as a hanging sign on a blustery day.
The sun as bright as lemons on a tree.
The houses are as old as my great grandma.
The birds' voices, as loud as my next door-neighbour's stereo.
The grip on the sea as good as my mum's grip on my dog's lead.
Can you imagine my favourite place?

Stephanie McKever (13)
Stantonbury Campus, Purbeck

The Classroom

Children and text books everywhere,
In the corner there's a blue fluffy chair.

Big posters on the wall with borders round them all,
Shapes and sizes, the children all call.

Hero wrappers, water bottles, tables and chairs,
In the cupboard there's a fluffy teddy bear.

Tape player, times tables, drawers everywhere,
Teacher's laptop on the spare chair.

The whiteboard shines,
The clock says quarter to nine.

The sun shines brightly
And everyone runs outside.

Emily Bowman (11)
Stoke-by-Nayland Middle School, Stoke-by-Nayland

A Storm
(Inspired by Valley Ranches 'Evening Storm')

Clouds
Turn grey,
Rain begins to come down hard,
Thunder strikes again,
Then all is quiet once more,
But the gentle patter of rain.

Then out of nowhere a flash booms
And a rumble of thunder is heard,
You can see the wave break against the rocks,
Another flash of yellow passes my eyes,
A tree falls down with a crack near me!

Olivia Stringer (11)
Stoke-by-Nayland Middle School, Stoke-by-Nayland

The Big Bad Bedroom

Cups as green as a leaf,
Hamster stuff which smells like beef,
The cricket bat in the corner.
The radiator keeping my room even warmer,
The window in the bedroom wall.
My chest of drawers is very tall,
My marbles are on the floor
And my folders block the bedroom door.
I take my books for a ride,
But I left the strap untied.
My TV is very fuzzy,
Which makes me extremely buzzy.
If you enter the big bad room
You will soon be consumed!

Jack Short (12)
Stoke-by-Nayland Middle School, Stoke-by-Nayland

A Traffic Jam
(Inspired by 'The Sound Collector' by Roger McGough)

Damn those stupid traffic jams
Hearing people snoring
Police cars speeding by the door
Oh, they're boring

The splashing of the water
The drilling of a drill
The chanting of some children
The turning of some mills

The droning of an aeroplane
The revving of a car
The tapping of a steering wheel
The hitting of a bar

The crying of a baby
The bibbing of a horn
The flashing of an ambulance
A farmer chewing corn.

Luke Wilding (11)
Stoke-by-Nayland Middle School, Stoke-by-Nayland

Creating A Storm

Sky
Darkens
Black clouds swell
Strike of lightning
Growl of thunder
Pitter-patter of rain
The water lever rises
Two ferocious bolts of lightning strike
Two buildings explode throwing rubble around
Remains swept away by rising currents
Screams of thoughts being crushed underneath the rubble
The wind twists as it creates an almighty tornado.

Jack Copping (12)
Stoke-by-Nayland Middle School, Stoke-by-Nayland

War
(Inspired by 'The Sound Collector' by Roger McGough)

The booming of the bombs.
The banging of the guns.
The shrieking of children,
Which are having no fun.

The crashing of the planes.
The revving of the trucks.
The squelching of mud,
As they walk through the muck.

The ringing of the alarm.
The chugging of the train.
The smashing from the tank.
The patter of the rain.

The screaming of the people.
The splashing of the ships.
The roaring of the fire.
The frying of the chips.

Michael Faulkner (11)
Stoke-by-Nayland Middle School, Stoke-by-Nayland

The Countryside
(Inspired by 'The Sound Collector' by Roger McGough)

The chiming of the church bell
The barking of the dog
The cooing of the pigeon
The foxes full of fear

The playing of the foxes
The screaming of the pheasant
The shouting of the magpie
The view is always pleasant

The whooping of the hunt
The squawking of the crows
The nibbling of the squirrels
And my dog's slimy nose.

Andrew Carter (12)
Stoke-by-Nayland Middle School, Stoke-by-Nayland

The Zoo Sound Collector
(Inspired by 'The Sound Collector' by Roger McGough)

A stranger called this morning
Dressed all in black and grey
Put every sound into a bag
And carried them away!

The screeching of the monkey
The clapping of the seals
The roaring of the elephants
The lions need their meals

The sleeping of the tiger
The moaning bears awake
The gorillas punch and munch
The zebras eating cake

The angry dolphin splashes
The birds all hide away
The wolves will howl and howl
Until the break of day

A stranger called this morning
He didn't leave his name
Left us only silence
Life will never be the same!

Bill Younger (11)
Stoke-by-Nayland Middle School, Stoke-by-Nayland

Top Gear
(Inspired by 'Jamaica Market' by Agnes Maxwell-Hall)

Biggest, best show on cars,
Mercedes, Bentleys, Jaguars,
All the cars take a test,
Driven by a celebrity guest,
Funny presenters, weirdest facts,
It will take you to the max,
It is no ordinary tat,
All in sixty minutes flat.

Jack Clark (12)
Stoke-by-Nayland Middle School, Stoke-by-Nayland

Zoo
(Inspired by 'The Sound Collector' by Roger McGough)

The laughing of the monkey,
The roaring of the lion,
The squawking of the seals,
The shouting of the zookeeper, Brian.

The yelling of the children,
The spitting of the llama,
The crying of the babies,
The chuckling of the farmer.

The squawking of the parrot,
The chuffing of the kiddies' train,
The trampling of the elephant,
The pouring of the rain.

Jack Anger (11)
Stoke-by-Nayland Middle School, Stoke-by-Nayland

Recipe For A Perfect Friend

Begin with bags full of kindness,
This will make the mixture loyal for a lifetime.
Add a teaspoon of joy and tenderness,
Then an ounce of trust,
Mix with honesty for added sweetness
And next stir in forgiveness or loving
In order to be a good friend,
Bake for eternity
And serve with a sprinkle of fun.

Helen Clarke (11)
Stoke-by-Nayland Middle School, Stoke-by-Nayland

Argos
(Inspired by 'Jamaica Market' by Agnes Maxwell-Hall)

A mobile phone, golden ring
Karaoke to help you sing

Hairdryers and straighteners too
A bog brush to clean your loo

Bubble baths, ride-away skates
Sexy clothes, colourful plates

Pairs of boots, a sea-green shirt
Plus a matching mini skirt

Carpets, rugs and comfy beds
Somewhere nice to lay our heads.

Katherine Brown (11)
Stoke-by-Nayland Middle School, Stoke-by-Nayland

Tesco's
(Inspired by 'Jamaica Market' by Agnes Maxwell-Hall)

Peanut butter, cheesy spread
All taste great on fresh baked bread

Crisps, chocolate, toffee and sweets
Not a mother's choice of treats

Rice, fish, potatoes and peas
Fresh honey from buzzing bees

Pork chops, chicken, fresh cut ham
Tuna fish and mushy spam.

Billy Richards (12)
Stoke-by-Nayland Middle School, Stoke-by-Nayland

Londis
(Inspired by 'Jamaica Market' by Agnes Maxwell-Hall)

Fresh baked bread, white toilet roll,
Green Brussels sprouts, lumpy black coal.

Pink ham, multicoloured sweets,
Bright green grapes, freshly cut meats.

Oxo pots, orange carrots,
Fruits from places with lots of parrots.

Red cans of Coke, white mushrooms,
Pink sausages, shiny spoons.

Green apples, food for a cat,
Ruby-red jam, a blue mat.

Michael Boorman (12)
Stoke-by-Nayland Middle School, Stoke-by-Nayland

Tesco's
(Inspired by 'Jamaica Market' by Agnes Maxwell-Hall)

Low fat butter, chocolate spread
Frozen peas, spongy white bread

The fattening taste of butter
While you hear people mutter

You need shiny kitchen foil
You can smell the olive oil

You take the delicious peas
While you eat honey from bees

You can see ruby-red jam
As well as the fresh pink ham.

Fred Howe (12)
Stoke-by-Nayland Middle School, Stoke-by-Nayland

The Seasons!

Spring is as new as a newborn baby.
Spring brings showers as heavy as waterfalls.
Spring is when tiny lambs pop up like bubbles.

Summer is as hot as an oven when it is on full heat.
Summer is the time for beach activities.
Summer boils like water in a kettle.

Autumn's leaves swirl like clouds in the sky.
Autumn makes the year turn colder like a radiator when it is turned off.
Autumn's leaves are coloured like blazing flames.

Winter is as cold and dark as a dark cave.
Winter is as bitter as lemons and limes.
Winter's snow covers the world like a cold white blanket.

Lauren W & Charlotte O'Connor (11)
Stoke-by-Nayland Middle School, Stoke-by-Nayland

A Poem About Tesco's
(Inspired by 'Jamaica Market' by Agnes Maxwell-Hall)

Warm, crispy, tasty, brown bread,
With yummy chocolate spread.

Egg, bacon and ruby-red jam,
Yucky mushrooms and bright pink ham.

Apple juice, bags of tea,
Sticky honey from a bee.

Bags of pears on the table,
Nutritious information on the label.

If you go into the shop,
I'm sure you will blow your top!

Olivia Powling (11)
Stoke-by-Nayland Middle School, Stoke-by-Nayland

The Range
(Inspired by 'Jamaica Market' by Agnes Maxwell-Hall)

New Christmas decorations
And party invitations

Swimming pools, trampoline
Make-up and a magazine

Cushions, duvets and a bed
Make it comfy for your head

A nice garden, pots and plants
Go on, use them, take a chance

Towels and carpets, curtains too
Get a wardrobe just for you.

Samantha Ingram
Stoke-by-Nayland Middle School, Stoke-by-Nayland

My Home
(Inspired by 'The Sound Collector' by Roger McGough)

The creaking of the door,
The screaming of my mum.
The hissing of the kettle,
The cats purring like they're dumb.

The nibble from the crisps,
The CD player at full blast.
The popping of the popcorn,
My brother running very fast.

The splashing in my pool,
The screaming in my house.
The rumbling of my tummy,
The squeaking of the mouse.

Naomi Welfare (11)
Stoke-by-Nayland Middle School, Stoke-by-Nayland

Sweet Shop!
(Inspired by 'Jamaica Market' by Agnes Maxwell-Hall)

Sweets are everywhere - north, west, south,
Take them all - put them in my mouth!

Fudge, mints, liquorish sticks,
Dairy Milk, Mars and Twix.

Strawberry or apple bubblegum,
Every flavour, berry to plum.

Every corner covered in Crunchies,
Penny sweets and minty Munchies.

Sugary, sticky Jelly Tots,
Cadbury and Berty Bots.

Munchy, crunchy, chewy things,
Teddy bears and Haribo rings.

Dairy Milk and chocolate poo,
Loads of sweets and new ones too.

So many choices - lollies, Polos,
Toffee, bonbons, gum and Rolos.

Millions to look at - sweets galore,
Once you've gone, you'll be wanting more.

My favourite sweet is a jawbeaker,
What a fantastic job being a sweet maker!

Catherine Chapman (12)
Stoke-by-Nayland Middle School, Stoke-by-Nayland

Crowd

The trains screeched like a conductor's whistle.
The troops' voices whistled through the air like a glider.
The tanks rushed through the camp, sounding like the roar of a lion.
The sirens whined like a baby screaming for its milk.
The planes gliding high like an eagle.
The grenades exploding like microwave popcorn.
The gas crept like a ghost towards the camp.

Sean Bocking & Harry Series (12)
Stoke-by-Nayland Middle School, Stoke-by-Nayland

Seasons Poem

Beautiful flowers shooting out the ground
Like ghosts appearing from their graves,
Snowflakes falling like sugar being poured into your tea,
Children throwing snowballs like frozen comets into space,
The summer sun beaming down like a flaming piece of coal,
People walking on the crunching leaves
Like cornflakes in your mouth,
Lambs jumping like fluffy white clouds moving in the sky,
Children playing in the calm sea like a giant bubble bath,
The crooked trees towering over you like a gate
Swinging back and forth.

Ella Etheridge & Rosie Coot (11)
Stoke-by-Nayland Middle School, Stoke-by-Nayland

The Supermarket
(Inspired by 'Jamaica Market' by Agnes Maxwell-Hall)

Sweet, sweet toffee, chocolate milk
Feathery wheat, gowns of silk

Red tomatoes, sticky jam
Strong, smelly cheese, pink roast ham

Gold olive oil, shiny keys
Juicy meat, green garden peas

Strong black coffee, baby books
Bright kitchen foil, white coat hooks

Low fat butter, cheesy spread
Shiny apples, soft white bread.

Laura Moore (11)
Stoke-by-Nayland Middle School, Stoke-by-Nayland

The Seasons

In spring the juicy apples grow as big as your fist,
In summer the sun is like a blazing ball of fire,
In autumn the leaves are like crispy brown mud,
In winter the snow is like soft polar bear's fur,
In spring the flowers blossom like beautiful multicoloured butterflies,
In summer the grass turns as yellow as a ripe banana,
In autumn the leaves fly like a helicopter in a drastic emergency,
In winter the sun is like the dull grey moon,
In spring the leaves turn as green as Granny Smith apples,
In summer the sky is like the clear blue Mediterranean Sea,
In autumn the grass is like rich chocolate sauce,
In winter the coldness of the snow is as cold as a freezer.

Kerrie Boyes & Kristie Robinson (12)
Stoke-by-Nayland Middle School, Stoke-by-Nayland

Sainsbury's
(Inspired by 'Jamaica Market' by Agnes Maxwell-Hall)

Christmas puddings and mince pies,
Men's underwear, socks and ties.

Newspapers and magazines,
Spaghetti and tins of beans.

Juicy fruits and clotted cream,
Children playing, hear them scream.

Televisions and CDs,
Red tomatoes and green peas.

To the counter, time to pay,
That is all I have to say.

Harriet Bourner (11)
Stoke-by-Nayland Middle School, Stoke-by-Nayland

A Crowd Of Soldiers In The War

The war is a game
With fine soldiers in a crowd
And they are the counters
That make the sergeant proud

The crowd of soldiers huddled together
Like a pack of wolves heading into war
They're aiming for the enemy's core

The tanks attack like raging bulls
Then the men follow
Their fingers numb from the bitter wind
The trees are hollow

Bullets shoot like rockets
Then like from taps, blood spills
Its jagged ground
With new red hills

Gunshots from the soldiers
Their hands as cold as ice
They are playing a game
Just like rolling dice.

Joseph Kurtz & Danny Hurlock (11)
Stoke-by-Nayland Middle School, Stoke-by-Nayland

At The Pet Shop

Loads of cute tiny gerbils,
Cats coughing up fur balls,
From the hutch popped a rabbit,
The dogs had a strange habit,
The snake ate its frozen mouse,
The hamster slept in its house,
Out of the tank popped a fish,
Guinea pigs drank from their dish,
Someone opened the dog food,
It smelled like the cat had pooed.

Daniel McGuinness (11)
Stoke-by-Nayland Middle School, Stoke-by-Nayland

The Banger Racing Ground

The crashing of cars as they hit the stand
The crackling of flames above the roar of cranes
The stillness of the crowd, not even a rustle of popcorn
Everybody feared about their future career

As the shock subsided, a flock of birds flew above
The stand emptied like water draining from a basin
The people sounded like lions but the noise soon died.

Calum Gilbey (11)
Stoke-by-Nayland Middle School, Stoke-by-Nayland

Shopping At Tesco's
(Inspired by 'Jamaica Market' by Agnes Maxwell-Hall)

Fresh and spongy nutty bread,
Lots of peanut butter spreads,
Sticky toffee chocolate treats,
Chicken legs and fresh cut meats,
Ruby-red tomato soup,
Exercising plastic hoop,
Spicy chicken tikka curry,
Shop is closing better hurry,
Green bananas, apples that shine,
Alcoholic strong red wine.

Kerrie Boyes (12)
Stoke-by-Nayland Middle School, Stoke-by-Nayland

The Pet Shop

Lots of rabbits, nervous and scared
Spying on gerbils with brown hair
Snakes slithering for a mouse
Fishes were hiding in their house
Lots of pretty kitty cats
Tiny rats wearing nice straw hats.

Murray Cox (11)
Stoke-by-Nayland Middle School, Stoke-by-Nayland

Noises On A Farm
(Inspired by 'The Sound Collector' by Roger McGough)

The puffing of hard work,
The slamming of a stable door,
The patter of small feet
On a concrete floor.

The clucking from a chicken,
The rustling from some hay,
The bleating from a sheep
That just gave birth today.

The snorting from a pig,
The mooing from a cow,
The whining from a puppy
That just started to howl.

The cooing from a cockerel,
The munching from a goat,
The rumble from an engine
That just started to sail a boat.

All these simple sounds,
Of which we don't really care,
But what would we do
If those sounds weren't there?

Charis Boon
Stoke-by-Nayland Middle School, Stoke-by-Nayland

Royal Rumble

There's going to be some trouble tonight
Because of the Royal Rumble, that's right!
Step in the ring, reach beyond our understanding,
When the smoke is clear, I'll be the last man standing
Because there can only be one
Royal Rumble winner!

Connan Hammond (12)
Stoke-by-Nayland Middle School, Stoke-by-Nayland

One Night In The Pub
(Inspired by 'The Sound Collector' by Roger McGough)

The clicking of the pool cue,
The thudding of the balls.
The knocking of the 8,
The potting of them all.

The clashing of the glasses,
The men shouting, 'Cheers!'
The sipping of the Bud,
The man carrying beers.

The popping of the wine cork,
The dinging of the darts.
The crunching of the crisps,
The music from the charts.

Timothy Leach (12)
Stoke-by-Nayland Middle School, Stoke-by-Nayland

Shopping At Morrisons
(Inspired by 'Jamaica Market' by Agnes Maxwell-Hall)

Newly flavoured cheesy dips
Lovely, salty, tasty chips
Slimy eggs and fresh baked bread
Shiny apples, chocolate spread
Great pink ham and fatty lard
And a purple birthday card
Orange juice and fizzy pop
Special offer on a mop
Chocolate cake and Dairy Milk
And a square of silver silk!

Eloise Warren (11)
Stoke-by-Nayland Middle School, Stoke-by-Nayland

The Pegasus Dream

Roaming horses soaring through the sky
With feathered white wings, they gallop, they fly
Striding out their mighty powerful legs
I dream of them all, every night before bed
Whinny, neigh, the hard stamping of hooves
Impatient horses awaiting some food
Silky thick tails, soft grey coats
Much friendlier than most farm-charging goats
They race the wind as fast as they can
Then I decide to sleep, thinking what's my next dream plan.

Amy Young (12)
Stoke-by-Nayland Middle School, Stoke-by-Nayland

All In A Day At A Sweet Shop
(Inspired by 'Jamaica Market' by Agnes Maxwell-Hall)

Sharp golden lemon drops,
Fizzy brown cola pops.

Lovehearts and chocolate bars,
Gobstoppers, sherbet cars.

Long strawberry laces,
Tasty chocolate faces.

Multicoloured Smarties,
Packed for lots of parties.

Raspberry bubblegum,
Mixed with a sugar thumb.

All in a day at a sweet shop.

Georgia Drummond (12)
Stoke-by-Nayland Middle School, Stoke-by-Nayland

War
(Inspired by 'The Sound Collector' by Roger McGough)

The booming of a tank
The banging of the guns
The screaming of the people
War is never fun

Smashing of the bombs
The revving of a truck
Planes flying high
Houses crushed to muck

Cracking of wood
The shouting of adults
Roaring of sirens
This truck has a catapult

People laying roses
The chugging of trains
While they left the town
With people left in pain.

Warwick Marshall (12)
Stoke-by-Nayland Middle School, Stoke-by-Nayland

Storm

Sky darkens
Black clouds swell
Heavy rain comes
The thunder's rumble
Makes the children scream
Finally the lightning strikes
And wakes up the animals
Once it had gone, a red sky appeared
Morning arisen, the sun was bright at sea
People went to the beach to have a nice swim.

Freddie Brasted-Watts (11)
Stoke-by-Nayland Middle School, Stoke-by-Nayland

Mornings!
(Inspired by 'Jamaica Market' by Agnes Maxwell-Hall)

Make-up, carpet, window place
Wind chimes, hair on pillowcase

Pictures, photos, big hard books
Tables, mirror, oh don't look!

Scrunchies, hair bands, teddy's bed
There I am hungrily fed

Handbag, hi-fi, strike a pose
Shoes, paper, sexy clothes

Quietly sleeping in my cover
Bang! Bang! There's my mother!

Molly Broughton (12)
Stoke-by-Nayland Middle School, Stoke-by-Nayland

The Sound Collector
(Inspired by 'The Sound Collector' by Roger McGough)

The cheering of the fans
The drumming of the bands
The whistling when they score
The eating when they bore
The shouting when they run
The clapping when they're done
The banging of the scrum
The cheering when they've won
The singing at the team
The booing of they're mean.

James Hazell (11)
Stoke-by-Nayland Middle School, Stoke-by-Nayland

The Sound Collector
(Based on 'The Sound Collector' by Roger McGough)

*'A stranger called this morning,
Dressed all in black and grey,'*
Put everything into a bag
And carried it away.

The whispering of the pupils
As the teacher speaks,
The rustling of book pages,
The pattering of feet.

The tapping of the pen lids,
The ticking of the clock,
The typing of computer keys
As the doors unlock.

The scribbling of the pencils,
The knocking on the door,
The coughing of the children
As they fetch books from the floor.

The music of the laptop,
The sliding of the trays,
All the children working
As the calming music plays.

The talking of the teacher
As the lessons come to a stop,
The shouting of the kiddies
As the lids of pens go *pop!*

*'A stranger called this morning,
He didn't leave his name,
Left us only silence,
Life will never be the same.'*

Maddie Lingi (11)
Stoke-by-Nayland Middle School, Stoke-by-Nayland

The Sea
(Inspired by 'The Sea' by James Reeves)

The sea is an angry lion,
Lying and waiting all day,
Looking for its prey.
Hear the lion roar,
Feeding on some more.

Early morning the beast awakes,
With the patter of his paws,
The earth quakes.
The lion is playful,
Rolling on the floor,
The sound he makes is like
The slamming of a door.

Furious and angry,
Coughing up stones,
Like he's about to spit out his bones.
But in the summer,
The beast calms down,
Almost like the king has lost his crown.

Hunter Wallis (11)
Stoke-by-Nayland Middle School, Stoke-by-Nayland

Forming A Fight

Look.
Mean looks.
Standing still.
Raising their fist.
Taking position.
Fists hitting really hard.
Hard kicks hitting bony shins.
Large crowds forming to watch.
Crowds start chanting names to support them.
Dark bruises appearing over bodies.
Fight that out of control that dark red blood appears.

Matthew Haggett (12)
Stoke-by-Nayland Middle School, Stoke-by-Nayland

Sweet Shop
(Inspired by 'Jamaica Market' by Agnes Maxwell-Hall)

Chocolate buttons, strawberry lace,
Children run like in a race.
Fizzy sherbet, apple juice,
Cherry drops and chocolate mousse.

White Maltesers and Iced Gems,
Butterscotch and M&Ms.
Dolly Mixture, toffee, fudge,
Melted chocolate turned to sludge.
Lemon sherbet, chocolate limes,
Dairy Milk and lots of Dimes.
Flying saucers, sugar mice,
Popping candy that tastes nice.
Popcorn, Revels, candy sticks,
Lollipops go very quick.
We have sweets of every hue,
Every taste for me and you.

Alice Catchpole (11)
Stoke-by-Nayland Middle School, Stoke-by-Nayland

Home
(Inspired by 'The Sound Collector' by Roger McGough)

The banging of the door
The rumbling of the train
The creak of the hinge
The ticking of my brain

The moaning of my brother
The barking of my dog
The groaning of my dad
The blinding of the fog

The rustling of the leaves
The slurping of milk
The patter of my feet
The softness of silk.

Kristina Elkin (11)
Stoke-by-Nayland Middle School, Stoke-by-Nayland

The Sound Collector
(Based on 'The Sound Collector' by Roger McGough)

*A stranger called today
Dressed all in black and grey
Put every sound into a bag
And carried them away*

He followed me to school
And this is what he heard
The scraping of the chair
The sniffing of the nerd

The thudding of children's feet
As they charge down the stair
The shouting of the teacher
The excitement of the pupils as they wait for the fair

The whispering of Year 8s as assembly begins
The hoarse voice of the teacher
The screeching of the violins

The *oops* of the little girl
As she knocks over the jug
The glaring of the dinner lady
The smashing of the mug

The ticking of the clock
As the kids urge it on
The pleasing sound of the bell
As the kids pull a con

*A stranger called today
He didn't leave his name
Left us only in silence
Life will never be the same.*

Florence Burdall Goodchild (11)
Stoke-by-Nayland Middle School, Stoke-by-Nayland

Humans

All different heights,
They walk around proud and straight.
There are lots and lots
Of these mysterious creatures,
Stiff and tall like robots.
They talk in a weird but wonderful language
And eat everything they can.
Some are of large build, some are tiny,
They fight their own species just to be the leader,
They can be powerful and destructive.
They all look different,
They can live anywhere and
They keep us animals as pets!
They build their houses on our land
Kick us out of our homes,
And they eat us,
The pigs, cows, rabbits, sheep and many more.
A small portion of these creatures
Are nice to us,
The birds and the bees,
They protect us from the dangerous ones,
They build boxes for our nests,
Look after our habitats
And give us food in the cold.
These creatures are just confusing,
They never make their minds up!

Chloe Chapman (11)
Stoke-by-Nayland Middle School, Stoke-by-Nayland

Football Match
(Inspired by 'The Sound Collector' by Roger McGough)

The cheering of the fans
The thump of the ball
The shouting of the goalkeeper
The line-up of the wall

The crying of the striker
The singing of the fans
The moaning of the manager
The supporters facing bans

The yelling of the supporters
The players getting hacked
The mumbling of the captain
The manger getting sacked.

Ricci Powell (11)
Stoke-by-Nayland Middle School, Stoke-by-Nayland

Bonfire

The bonfire flames lick and flicker and hiss
Like
Tongues of ravenous wolves
Like
A tiger's crouch and leap
Like
Bright serpents with venomous fangs
Like
A luminous, never-ending flame
Like
A blinding phoenix flame
Like
Making shapes in the smoky air
Like
A bit of sun fallen from the sky
Getting brighter and brighter and then gone.

Elliot Allan (12)
Stoke-by-Nayland Middle School, Stoke-by-Nayland

The River Is A Snake

The river is a slithery snake
Long and windy
Slithering down the valley
With its hissing and winding
It never will stop flowing
Down the riverbed
And *hiss, hiss, hiss*
As he slides into the distance
Wiggling his tail behind him

Then when it turns dark and cold
And the moon is out and bright
He keeps going smoothly
Splashing his tail
And curving his body

But when it's freezing cold
He comes to a halt
He is frozen and still
No more wiggling or moving
He lies there silently
Until the sun comes out again.

Leonie Dolling (12)
Stoke-by-Nayland Middle School, Stoke-by-Nayland

Home
(Inspired by 'The Sound Collector' by Roger McGough)

The screaming of my sister
The purring of my cat
The clanking of the garage
The swinging of my bat
The shouting of my mum
The squeaking of the door
The splashing of the shower
The creaking of the floor.

Jack Furssedonnc (12)
Stoke-by-Nayland Middle School, Stoke-by-Nayland

A Poem About War
(Inspired by 'The Sound Collector' by Roger McGough)

The booming of a bomb,
The report of a rifle,
The rumbling of a tank,
The crashing of the Eiffel.

The crying of children,
The tumbling of men,
The vibration of guns,
The neighing of horses in their pens.

The whistling of a mortar,
The slamming of a door,
The shouting of men,
This is all about war.

Christian Clarke (11)
Stoke-by-Nayland Middle School, Stoke-by-Nayland

Zoo
(Inspired by 'The Sound Collector' by Roger McGough)

The roaring of the tiger.
The chattering of the monkey.
The howling of the wolf.
The braying of the donkey.

The singing of the lark.
The purring of the cat.
The growling of the bear.
The squeaking of the bat.

The ramming of the rhino.
The calling of the zookeeper, Brian.
The screaming of the hyena.
The roaring of the lion.

Joseph Butcher (11)
Stoke-by-Nayland Middle School, Stoke-by-Nayland

Military Airport
(Inspired by 'The Sound Collector' by Roger McGough)

The shouting of the sergeant
The stomping of the troops
The hammering of the mechanics
The marching of the groups

The chattering of the guns
The shouting of the men
The humming of the propellers
The emptying of the den

The roaring of the Harriers
The loading of the guns
The power-hungry tanks
The slaughter of mothers' sons.

George Killick (12)
Stoke-by-Nayland Middle School, Stoke-by-Nayland

The Noisy Zoo
(Inspired by 'The Sound Collector' by Roger McGough)

The roaring of a lion
The hissing of a snake
The monkeys chattering noisily
A lot of sounds to make

The howling of a wolf
The clucking of a hen
The braying of a donkey
The talking of the men

The laughing of the kids
The oinking of the pigs
The quacking of the ducks
The people chewing figs.

Dean Riley (11)
Stoke-by-Nayland Middle School, Stoke-by-Nayland

War
(Inspired by 'The Sound Collector' by Roger McGough)

The booming of the bomb
The blare of the siren
The scream of the children
The report of rifles firin'

The rumbling of the tanks
The chattering of a machine gun
The wailing of the injured
It's just Hitler having fun

The crashing of falling buildings
The crackling of the fire
The stamping of marching feet
The howl of the plane as it climbs higher.

Robbie Waters (12)
Stoke-by-Nayland Middle School, Stoke-by-Nayland

Metaphor

Try and guess what it is!

It is an angry dragon,
Roaring as it thrashes around.
Foaming at the mouth,
It pulls at any unsuspecting victim.
The dragon claws at the sandy banks,
Pulling back the sand and stone.
Its tail crashes against the rocks,
As it screams out in hunger.
It pads up and down the shingle,
Looking for food
And as it gets dark,
It curls its tail round itself.
Snoring gently it bobs up and down,
People timidly creeping up to it,
But fall back at the sound of a roar.

Lucy Ratcliffe (11)
Stoke-by-Nayland Middle School, Stoke-by-Nayland

Sweetie Shop
(Inspired by 'Jamaica Market' by Agnes Maxwell-Hall)

Liquorish, buttons, gummy bears
Jelly Tots, toffee and éclairs

Pots of Skittles with rainbow taste
None of these will go to waste

Polos, Mars, Maltesers too
Flavoured lollies coloured blue

Gobstoppers, laces, penny sweets
Gum and Minstrels, lovely treats

Chocolate fudge and ice cream
Cream eggs, Galaxy, also Dream

Haribo makes all kinds of things
Maoam, hearts, dummies, rings

Cola bottles, candy strips
Fizzy lollies and their dips

Tutti Fruities, crisps and all
If you don't buy these, you'll be a fool

Flying saucers, Crunchies, yum
All of these to fill my tum!

Alice Dodd (11)
Stoke-by-Nayland Middle School, Stoke-by-Nayland

The Lion And Albert (My Version)
(Inspired by 'The Lion and Albert' by Marriot Edgar)

I was lying there minding my business,
When some people came up to my cage.
The kid started poking my ear
And then I swelled up with rage.

I shoved my paw through the bars
And pulled the kid inside.
Into my mouth I placed him,
But not very nice was his hide.

Alex Leon (11)
Stoke-by-Nayland Middle School, Stoke-by-Nayland

Animals
(Inspired by 'Jamaica Market' by Agnes Maxwell-Hall)

Lion roaring, it's the king.
Penguins swimming, flapping wings.
Cheetahs running, fast as lightning.
Grizzly bear, really frightening.
Monkeys swinging from tree to tree.
Giraffes explore and roam free.
Tropical fish dart in and out.
Gorillas grumpy, lips in a pout.
Flamingos are pink and stand on one leg,
Waiting all day to be fed.
Wild geese waddle near.
All the children cry with fear.
Seals perform amazing tricks.
While dolphins perform acrobatic flicks.
On the pond the bugs all sleep.
While frogs hop about doing giant leaps.
Animals, animals, big and small.
Animals, animals, short and tall.

Ava Allan (12)
Stoke-by-Nayland Middle School, Stoke-by-Nayland

Night Sky

The night sky is a giant blanket covering up the sun
The stars are the sun peeking through the little holes in the blanket

The moon is a torch shining through the blanket

The planets are the stains on the blanket that can't come out
The blanket is there for protection from the sun

As the blanket is put over, everyone is put into a deep sleep
And they don't wake up till it is removed
When they are asleep, they leave their troubles behind them

When the blanket is removed, everyone is awoken
By a beautiful sunrise.

Georgina Howe (11)
Stoke-by-Nayland Middle School, Stoke-by-Nayland

Little Red Riding Hood

When Little Red Riding Hood went to town,
She was in her best red velvet gown,
She went to see her sick grandmother,
Who was wrapped up in bed in a huge cover,
With her, in a basket she did take,
Crisps and orange juice and jaffa cakes,
She made her way through the crowded streets,
Being trampled on by tons of feet,
She finally arrived at Granny's house,
She was up in bed, drinking Grouse,
It surely was not Granny there,
Instead there was a massive bear,
'Hey, Granny,' she shouted in alarm,
Before she knew it, she was in the bear's arms,
'Oh Granny, oh Granny, oh those eyes,
I should call the FBI.
Oh Granny, you have such huge ears,
Also need them in my career,
Oh my, Granny what big teeth you've got,
When you're chewing toffee you must be red-hot.'
Little Red Riding Hood was eaten real fast,
Also with the flower vase,
She still remains there to this day,
Never found, to her dismay.

Anja Donnellan (11)
Stoke-by-Nayland Middle School, Stoke-by-Nayland

Recipe For A Perfect Friend

Begin with bags full of niceness,
This will make the mixture friendly and helpful.
Add a teaspoon of kindness
And an ounce of love, mix with fun for added happiness.
Bake for 13 years
To make a perfect friend.

Sophie Faulkner (13)
Stoke-by-Nayland Middle School, Stoke-by-Nayland

The Funny Fish Tank

The goldfish splash about,
Like small beams of fire
And swimming stone drunk,
The beer fish get higher.

Perilous piranhas,
Bite off more than they can chew,
Then swordfish and clownfish
Want to return to the deep blue.

A small toy castle,
Inhabited by cod and pike,
A long electric eel,
Powers a miniature trike.

Many crazy fish,
Do other human-like things,
From breeding pet animals
And forging golden rings.

So now you truly know
About the funny fish tank,
With business fish
And ones that work in banks.

I hope you can see it,
At least once every few years
And see the little fish,
Breeding pigs and deer.

Ross Britcher (11)
Stoke-by-Nayland Middle School, Stoke-by-Nayland

A Stranger Came To My Castle
(Inspired by 'The Sound Collector' by Roger McGough)

A stranger came to the castle,
All dressed up in black
And picked up all the sound
And put it in a bag.

The neighing of a horse,
The calling of the lord.

The clashing of the blacksmith,
Making an iron sword.

The chopping of a head on a wooden block,
Gone to a better place.
The hanging of a felon,
The pain to see in his face.

The heat of molten metal,
In the armourer's guild,
Behind the walls of the siege factory,
A battering ram they build.

The creaking of a drawbridge,
As the chains do turn,
The crackling of the fire,
As the witches burn.

That's the myth of the castle,
That was muted of all sound,
Now all that remains standing,
Is an earthen mound.

Adam Todd (12)
Stoke-by-Nayland Middle School, Stoke-by-Nayland

The Sea
(Inspired by 'The Sea' by James Reeves)

The sea is a ferocious bull
Large and grey
It flows ragingly all day
With bashing teeth and ragged jaws
Looking for its next victim

Sulking for its prey
He's angry in distress
Hour after hour
Licking his greasy jaws

When the wind is roaring
He gets to his feet
Sniffing and snuffling
He groans and growls long and loud
He relaxes on the sandy shore
So peaceful
Suddenly there is no sound.

Alex Stevens (12)
Stoke-by-Nayland Middle School, Stoke-by-Nayland

Linking - Couplets

Flowers, pollen, bees, honey,
Shops, sale, profit, money.

Cost, notes, pounds, price,
Receipt, change, numbers, dice.

Cube, corners, angles, degrees,
Weather, wind, trees, leaves.

Orange, round, pips, skin,
Peel, separate, eat, bin.

Lucy Cowlin (11)
Stoke-by-Nayland Middle School, Stoke-by-Nayland

Weather

Like a thin layer of smoke
Drifting round being blown
By a dark hand
Sweeping the tobacco smell

Like an iceberg steaming
Slowly moving off course
The clouds change colour
Like a confused chameleon

Gradually getting darker
And falling apart
Into many water crystals
Like an exploding can

The sky darkens fast
And roars like an angry tiger
It disappears behind
A great cloud army ready for battle

The sky eventually clears
Sunshine emerges from the dark
Like a floodlight beaming
Stabbing the clouds on the way down.

Rhys Taylor (12)
Stoke-by-Nayland Middle School, Stoke-by-Nayland

Robins!

Robins flying through the cold winter's snow,
Singing songs of joy.
But one little robin was left on his own,
Singing a sad little song.
Till Rudolph popped out of the sky
With presents galore,
Sad little robin was sad no more.

Samantha Gammage (11)
Stoke-by-Nayland Middle School, Stoke-by-Nayland

Imagine

Imagine the sea as a teacher
Imagine the power concealed
Imagine how this deadly menace
Can terrorise for all eternity

Imagine the sea on a stormy day
Imagine the sea roaring in angriness
As it punishes the wrong

Imagine it on quiet days as in May or June
Imagine the tenderness of the calming waters
Sleeping . . . sleeping . . .

Imagine it sleeping so quietly . . . so quietly
Until it wakes in its fury to kill

Imagine the sea as a teacher
Imagine the power concealed
Imagine how it teaches a new thing every day.

Samuel Pentney (12)
Stoke-by-Nayland Middle School, Stoke-by-Nayland

Metaphor Poem
(Inspired by 'The Sea' by James Reeves)

The sea is a fierce pig,
Large and fat,
Awaiting its first victim of the day.
He lies down snoring being lazy and fat,
Sulking and trying to get attention,
Bashing against the rock,
In anger as he gets distressed.
The rocks begin to quake
And the ground begins to shake,
The wind whistling in the air
As the pig answers in snorts,
On the quiet days he lays silent,
For one day he will be dead.

Anthony Waugh (12)
Stoke-by-Nayland Middle School, Stoke-by-Nayland

The Sea
(Inspired by 'The Sea' by James Reeves)

The sea is a war taking millions, never to return them.
The sea is an angry lion roaring.
The sea is a never-ending lake.
The sea is a mighty power hidden by a calm, misleading surface.
The sea is a hiding place of giants.
The sea is a sanctuary for mystical creatures.
The sea is a never-ending food supply.
The sea is a lonely wolf howling for the company of its own kind.
The sea is a good friend and a deadly enemy.
The sea is an asset and an obstacle helping and hurting.
The sea is an opportunity that many have found.
The sea is a source of pure power.
The sea is a weapon more destructive than is imaginable.
The sea is a graveyard.
The sea is a home.

Sam Faithfull (12)
Stoke-by-Nayland Middle School, Stoke-by-Nayland

Owl

A stalker of the night,
Gliding through a black abyss,
His wings, paddles in a raging river,
He lands on a green airstrip when he spots a victim.

Now a racer of the night,
He leads his prey into danger,
A tiger, he readies his pounce,
But by an inch, the hammer blows a miss.

Chris Heard (11)
Stoke-by-Nayland Middle School, Stoke-by-Nayland

The Three Pigs' Rap

This is a rap about three little pigs
So listen with your big old ears

They were at their home all warm and snug
When a wolf came up, he looked like a thug

One went to a house of straw
Shame he couldn't afford no more

Another ran to a house of sticks
While the other built a house of bricks

The house of bricks was as hard as rocks
And the other ones were as light as socks

The wolf walked past with a smile on his face
He looked at the pigs and wondered how they'd taste

He asked the straw pig if he could come in
But Piggy said, 'Not by the hair on my chin.'

So he puffed and he puffed and blew the house in
And ate the pig, for his din-din

It tasted very good, so he wanted one more
And the one other piggy he saw

The next house was built of sticks
'Ah,' he said, 'it's a pick 'n' mix.'

He ate the pig and his tum was full
And thought he should run a bacon stall

There was one more pig that he needed to eat
This little pig was full of meat

He couldn't blow the house down and he went bright red
So he jumped down the old chimney instead

He looked down the chimney and screamed with fear
As he fell in the boiling water and the pig gave a cheer

That's the end of our rap
So give us a clap.

Ashley Brandon (12)
Stoke-by-Nayland Middle School, Stoke-by-Nayland

The Lion And Albert
(Inspired by 'The Lion and Albert' by Marriot Edgar)

I was lying there minding my business,
When some people came up to my cage,
There was a ma, a pa and a son,
The son was dressed smartly in beige.

At first the boy looked scared,
Then he began to calm down,
Then he stuck his stick in my ear,
I shot him a real sharp frown!

So I grabbed the kid and pulled him in
And swallowed him down in one,
Then Pa came over and said,
'What on earth have you done to my son?'

Then Ma said about Albert,
'What's wrong with the world today?'
Then I said, quite peacefully,
'Why, I think I have flushed him away.'

My keeper came over annoyed
And said, 'You mean little lion you,
We're going to cut you open,
There's nothing else we can do.'

They slished and they slashed with a chainsaw
And when they found Albert, he was dead,
But it is a very sad ending,
For so was I, they could not get me repaired . . .

Sam Trafford (12)
Stoke-by-Nayland Middle School, Stoke-by-Nayland

Tongue Twister

He heard her heel on the hilltop
Her heel he heard on the hilltop
He held her hand to the hilltop
Her hand he held to the hilltop.

Natalie Sullivan (12)
The John Bramston School, Witham

The Hunter

He is a hunter
building his silky, beautiful den.
Everyone bows before him,
for he is the king.
No one dares to cross him,
for they know they will be hunted down.
The hunter is crafty,
his den is a masterpiece.
An innocent creature comes passing by
and sees a glistening in the distance.
The creature is curious and is attracted near,
what a deadly mistake.
Before he knows it,
it's trapped and can't break free.
Something big and black comes slinking towards the creature
and the poor little thing becomes paralysed with fright.
The hunter is hungry.
The hunter starts to rip the creature's soft flesh into shreds
and begins to enjoy a wonderful feast.
As he looks along the garden,
all the creatures bow before him.
For he is king,
king of the garden,
king of the world,
the spider.

Jade Markwell (14)
The John Bramston School, Witham

Valentine's Day

Valentine's Day is a special time of year,
Especially for the ones you love and hold dear,
Give her roses, flower posies,
Chocolate and teddies too,
It's a day on which you say
'I love you!'

Jade Peters (14)
The John Bramston School, Witham

Summer Love

Looking out the window
The birds sing a peaceful tune
As the sun shines upon the sand
The sea sweeps backwards and forwards
Across the golden carpet
Like blue ribbons in the wind.

A young man at the step,
Looking up at me, high in a castle,
Upon whom my eyes do fix,
His hair moving in the wind,
His eyes daring and bright,
Looks upon me with a smile
From one's heart.

He calls me as the evening arrives,
Love is all around as we sit on the beach
In the summer heat,
As we move closer, our lips touch
For a moment or two,
Have I found my true love this summer?

Hannah Gorrie (15)
The John Bramston School, Witham

Cars

I got the nitro button to press
My car is designed to impress
My spoiler is suped up
Whilst you and your car are locked up
Carbon fibre parts
Your car isn't worth them.

Richard Clunie (14)
The John Bramston School, Witham

My Feline Friends

Cute and nice, are rare to find.
Evil and mean, are known to hide.
Scary and cruel, are left to one side,
But remember, they're always kind.
Deadly but nice is a common one,
Much more known as the Devil's son.
Trickery is a black cat's charm,
Witches have trouble keeping them calm.
Pure white cats live in the clouds,
Often purring to whoever's around.
Finally there's the ginger cat,
Who is too horrible to describe.
So just turn around at the sight
Of a ginger cat or any as a matter of fact.

Amanda Green (12)
The John Bramston School, Witham

My Best Friends

Friends are someone special
to look up to when you're down
even if you have a frown
they always make you smile.

Friends are someone special
even if you break up
and you don't talk to each other
eventually you'll make up.

Friends are someone special
when you play out
if you get badly injured
they're always there to help.

Friends are someone special
even when you're going out
you should still respect them
as they would do to you.

Darren Briley (12)
The John Bramston School, Witham

Movies

Movies, movies, all so fun
I like almost every one

Action and comedy
Thrillers too
I hate love films
They're really dull
War and horror
Blood and gore, dead people too
Are all the things that make me watch the whole way through

DVD, videos, cinema too
These are how and where I watch them through

I'll watch them until I'm done
As long as I'm always having fun.

Patrick McDonagh (13)
The John Bramston School, Witham

A Football Ballad

I was on the train,
To watch a football match.
I felt great,
But it was a two hour ride.

They were coming out of the tunnel,
They were getting the crowd going.
Kick-off has started,
It's going to be a great game.

Fans roar on and on,
To get the best out of the players.
Every goal that's scored, there's a cheer,
The fans wave their scarves and flags.

Now the match finishes
And I will start my journey home.
There's a train delay,
I hope I will be home today!

Carl Walker (13)
The John Bramston School, Witham

The Big City

It's a dark and gloomy night,
In the big city.
The lamp posts are on
And the streets are empty.

The water is like a mirror,
Reflecting the big city.
The sun is down, the moon is up,
All you can see is darkness.

The stars are up,
The lamp posts are working.
If they weren't bringing us some light,
We would be encased in darkness.

The buildings are big,
They cave you in,
Don't go down an alleyway
Or you'll be lost in the big city.

So many things,
A lot to do,
But you can get bored,
In the big city.

Charlie Newman (13)
The John Bramston School, Witham

Sunshine

M y friends come round
I nside, outside, playing about
C hildren in the swimming pool
H ot sunshine fills the air
A unties, uncles, coming to stay
E xcited children in the garden
L aughing, shouting, playing too
A ll in all, it's been a good summer.

Michaela Williamson (13)
The John Bramston School, Witham

Penguins

Penguins are cute,
Penguins are sweet,
They live in cold weather
And waddle their feet.

They're cuddly and small,
They live in the snow,
They waddle around,
Going to and fro.

I love to watch them swim,
As they dive down under the sea
And the way they walk around,
It's just like you and me.

I love almost everything about them
And if I could have a wish,
I would spend a day as a penguin,
Except I don't like fish.

Rachel Challis (13)
The John Bramston School, Witham

Summer

Summer is great
It is so much fun
We can get up late
No more school work to get done

We can go to the beach
Meet our friends at the park
No school for six weeks
Can stay out late after dark

The sun is hot
I like it a lot.

Sadie Coe (14)
The John Bramston School, Witham

Gymnastics

G reat pride and joy when your name is called to receive your medal from the podium.
Y our parents are amazed by your outstanding effort.
M ind-exhausting competitions.
N ot always ready, so it becomes dangerous.
A dmirers inspired by your flexibility and strength.
S teady hands mean a steady mind.
T riple back sumi perfectly finished.
I nspirational moves to raise money for charity.
C ompetitive all the time.
S omersaults are the perfect end to a routine.

Danielle Williamson (13)
The John Bramston School, Witham

1-1 At Half-Time

Ref blows the whistle
Blues kick off
Back to the midfielder
Who boots it straight over the top
Reds' defenders fight for the ball
It's a thrown-in
Foul throw, Blues' manager's head
Nearly goes pop
They really want to win
Reds keep tackling
Striker shoots, goalie dives
It's a goal, crowd goes wild
Beeep!
Reds use the same tactics
Handball by a Blue, it's a penalty
The keeper's a calamity
1-1 at half-time.

Rosie Sontag (13)
The John Bramston School, Witham

Holidays

I was on my way to Turkey,
Where the water's very murky,
I was excited as a monkey
Cos Turkey's very funky!

Chorus
Holidays, holidays, oh such good times,
Holidays, holidays, oh such sad times,
Holidays, holidays, can be painful,
Holidays, holidays, just be grateful.

Finally we got on the plane,
But my sister went insane,
The flight was ten hours,
Only if I had powers, so this plane could fly for less hours.

Chorus

We landed where the weather was hot,
So hot, people started to rot,
I got on the boiling, baking coach,
Then out came a cockroach.

Chorus

We reached our hotel,
So tired we fell,
Unpacked our stuff,
But stopped cos we had enough!

Chorus

Next day we went to a theme park,
We waited for a ride in the dark,
My brother came off, scared,
He looked at me and glared . . .

Daniel Sheehan (14)
The John Bramston School, Witham

Snakes!

S lithering, making its move, readying itself
N ot caring, its heart as cold as its blood
A s it strikes it infects, poisoning its prey, losing grip on life
K illing its food, killing it quick, killing its prey
E ating its catch quick, all at once its life's taken

C atching and killing, as cold as ice
O ver the dunes it slithers and slides
B ringing its trail of death wherever it goes
R avaging the lives of those it seeks
A gonising pain from its venom

V icious as it strikes
I n waiting for its prey to come
P erilous to those who are found by it
E verlasting fear struck into those that meet it
R eadying for its next meal.

Andrew Husband (13)
The John Bramston School, Witham

Piggy

Piggy is yellow
Piggy is white
Piggy gives me such a fright

When she's at school
She acts the fool

When she's at home
She doesn't moan

She likes to take a bath
And have a laugh

Now piggy has had her fun
Now she's going in my bacon bun.

Warren Potgieter (14)
The John Bramston School, Witham

Computer Gaming

C ompletely obsessed
O n the ball
M ore kills than the rest
P ad is in your hands, you don't want to let go
U ltimate player of the game
T rash talking to your friends
E verlasting fun
R eady to go kick some butt

G oing for the win
A pproaching for the kill
M oan of a shoot, you are dead
E verything was done for nothing.

Warren Pennock (14)
The John Bramston School, Witham

Spain!

Spain is very hot,
I liked being there a lot,
It is very fun,
Sunbathing in the sun.

Spain is very carefree,
A great place for a shopping spree.
The food is very nice,
Although it is mostly rice.

The sea is as clear blue as the sky,
When you look at it, it makes you go, my, my, my.
I loved lying on the beach and getting a tan,
It was like laying on a frying pan.

Melissa Peckham (14)
The John Bramston School, Witham

Upton Park On A Match Day

The atmosphere at Upton Park
Is tense and anxious here.
For if West Ham win tonight,
They play premiership football next year.

A predominant pass from Reo-coker
Is thumped towards the goal.
As Harewood headers to Sheringham,
With all his heart and soul.

As rain disgorges onto the pitch,
The players' confidence grows.
A potential high Zamora has a shot
And into the net it goes.

The encouragement and the applause,
The shouts, the screams, the cheers.
All is forgotten at Upton Park,
For The Hammers are leading here.

The away fans of Sheffield United,
Look disgruntled and upset,
Some start moaning, others jeer
Because down the drain's their bet.

A sea of claret and blue in the stands,
Are dancing all warm-hearted,
As players celebrate on the pitch,
It's like it's just started.

But Sheffield don't give in so easy,
They push, they battle, they fight.
They keep on trying and have a shot
And boy, it was a sight!

Jim Walker sprawling to his left,
Punches the ball clear,
But Lindell was at the post,
To nod it in and cheer.

Sheffield fans explode and shout,
As their team sprint up the pitch.
West Ham look so plaintive,
They consider it a hitch.

As the final whistle goes here,
The ground is not alight,
The atmosphere is dull and grey
And not a pretty sight.

They drew one-all at Upton Park,
They won't be playing premier football.
There's always next year West Ham,
Good luck into the future.

Greg Cable (13)
The John Bramston School, Witham

Best Friend

Laughing, joking, having fun,
Sharing holidays in the sun.
Happily chatting in the park,
Out in the garden, in the dark.

Exciting fun comes round the bend,
Parties and sleepovers never end.
You will never forget how you met,
Even if you get into debt.

Friends, friends, loyal and true,
Even when you're down and blue.
To cheer you up and make you smile,
For you, they would run a mile.

Friends are worth more than gold,
That last until you get old.
As the summer passes into winter,
Friends can't hurt you like a splinter.

Dancing and playing games,
Inside when it rains.
Eating sweets and cakes,
That your friend's mum bakes.

Paris Smallbone (14)
The John Bramston School, Witham

About A Boy

We used to be in love,
We used to be one.
We used to be happy,
But now we are none.
Knowing you're with her,
Brings a tear to my eye.
Seeing you without me,
Makes me want to die.
All those years together,
Now all that time apart.
You think I'd be over you,
But you're still in my heart.
I don't want to cry anymore,
I don't want to spend those nights alone.
Why can't you come back to me?
So I don't have to moan.
I told you I loved you,
You told me you loved me.
It seemed like your heart was locked,
But I thought I had the key.
I know I'm the one who split us up,
That's a regret you cute little pup.
It's my fault, I shouldn't have left,
Boy, you're in my head all of the time,
Why can't you listen, it could work out fine.
We had so much love,
Where has that gone?
But maybe I should just try and move on
And face facts, that you are gone!

Hayley Drew (14)
The John Bramston School, Witham

The Goat

A goat
Is not a boat,
Nor does it try to be a coat
And it can't vote,
So a goat
Is not a boat,
Coat,
Neither can it vote
Because it's a goat!
If you wrote
A goat
A note,
The goat
Wouldn't read the note
That you wrote
To the goat,
That doesn't try to be a coat,
Because it's a goat,
If you were on a boat
And you had a goat
On your boat,
Then you pushed the goat
Off the boat,
Into a moat,
The goat
Wouldn't float
In the moat,
Where you threw the goat,
That can't vote,
Because it's a goat!

Ben Preca (14)
The John Bramston School, Witham

My Poem To You

I know you're not mine
But I wish you'd
Be my valentine

I love you
But you don't love me
And I will feel this way for eternity

I will see you
Forever and ever
But we will never be together

When we're sitting in French
I feel like we should be
On our own private bench

I wrote this poem, just for you
Because I want you
And my love for you is true.

Rick Webb (12)
The John Bramston School, Witham

I Don't Know

I really don't know what to do,

D ifficult to think of ideas,
O ver and over again, I'm thinking,
N othing comes to me.
T his poem writing is really difficult,

K nowing that
N o one else is struggling,
O nly me!
W ish I didn't have to do this!

Dean Flowers (15)
The John Bramston School, Witham

Winter Wonderland

It is the cold month of December
The month I just love
Christmas is coming
Snow as white as a dove
I am looking forward to
All the presents I will receive
Then it will be January
The good times will then leave

It is the cold month of January
The month I just hate
Christmas is over
Ice as slippery as a snake
Alarms in the morning
I must be awake
But soon it's my birthday
Ahh lots of cake.

Katie Hassain (12)
The John Bramston School, Witham

Love

Love, what is it?
Is it a word or does it have meaning?
Love is strong and should come from the heart,
Love is strong and shouldn't split you apart,
The love that people share should mean so much,
The love that people share should keep in touch,
Love, what is it?
Is it just a word or does it have meaning?

Jazmin Harrington (14)
The John Bramston School, Witham

Fireworks

When it comes around,
You know when the magic's about.
The *bang*, the *view*,
What a great sight to spend with you.

The *bang*, the *view*,
It makes me feel special
Or is it just standing next to you?
The *blue,* the *red,* the *white,* the *fright,*
Oh what a great night.

Remember, remember the 5th of November.

Mathew Brown (15)
The John Bramston School, Witham

Teachers

Teachers may be cool,
Teachers may be fun,
Some teachers think they are the best,
They think they're number one.

Teachers may be young,
Teachers may be old,
Some teachers may have hair,
Some teachers may be bald.

Teachers may be girls,
Teachers may be boys,
The teachers, they go mental,
When the kids make lots of noise.

Kayley Ager (14)
The John Bramston School, Witham

Morning Poem

I have got to get up today,
It is such a pain,
In the field I can hear the horses neigh
It's a Friday, yay!

I climb out of bed,
I put my hand on my head,
Oh, what a beautiful day,
Looking over the bay.

I tumble down the stairs,
I eat a juicy pear.

I jump into action,
Put on my outfit,
I bounce into the car
And off I go.

Katie Hutton (12)
The John Bramston School, Witham

Fireworks

The fifth of November
Is when the magic starts.
The sky lights up like magic stars,
Hands over the hearts,
When you jump from the *bang*.

Sparklers sparkling all around,
Black and white and coloured ones,
Circles in the sky.

Kalvin Monk (15)
The John Bramston School, Witham

My Holiday At Langdale

Vast mountains reach up to the sky
Whilst birds glide gently by
Lakes lay still and tranquil

Many people marching
The rest are just larking
Some are rowing

It was snowing
One winter's day
You heard all children laugh and play

The wind was blowing in our faces
A herd of sheep ran some races
People sleeping, rivers dreeping
This was the end of the day.

Daniel Cowell (13)
The John Bramston School, Witham

Autumn

The leaves are turning golden brown
And falling to the ground,
They crunch underneath our feet as we walk around,
The wind then sweeps them up again
And sends them twirling up into the air,
As I look out my window I see the leaves whirling round,
As I sit by the fire I get a warm feeling inside
And I tell myself it's autumn,
The best time of the year.

Yasmin Ledwell (14)
The John Bramston School, Witham

Like And Hate Subjects

I really like English
It is quite easy to finish
It's one of my best subjects
It's not one of the rejects

I also like art
It's easy to start
Another best subject
Not one I'd neglect

I really hate maths
I'd rather sit in a bath
It's much more fun
Eating a bun!

I also hate science
You have to sit in silence
I sit in the class
Hoping it will quickly pass.

Katie Sage (15)
The John Bramston School, Witham

The Classroom

C reativity, imagination,
L iterature placed on the walls,
A tmosphere so soulful,
S ight so still,
S ound so silent,
R eady to learn,
O ld stories treasured,
O pen minds,
M agnificent words.

Christina Moore (13)
The John Bramston School, Witham

A Waterfall Comes Crashing Down

A waterfall comes crashing down,
Splashing water all around,
Jumping in like a fool,
Diving in thinking you are cool,
Dirty water in the sea,
The depth coming to the knee.

People soaking in the bath,
Making little children laugh,
Put you plates in the sink,
Or nice cold water in your drink.

Charlie Jeffery (14)
The John Bramston School, Witham

Stars

Stars, stars, they shine so bright,
They make me see the moonlight,
The stars twinkle, twinkle so magically,
To not see them at night would be a tragedy.

The spiky twiglets on the stars,
Make me wonder, wonder and ask,
If they'll ever go away,
The night will be stolen, so I hope they stay.

The stars that gleam in the sky,
Make me blink as they twinkle by,
Stars shining brightly as can be,
Are they shining just for me?

Gemma Foxlow (12)
The John Bramston School, Witham

Valentine's Day

Valentine's Day is for love and joy
Just for that special boy
You love them dearly
They can see it clearly
You send them a card
Finding them the appropriate one is hard
On the day
You hope your troubles will blow away
You hope you get a card in return
But you never seem to get it!
Next year comes
You fiddle your thumbs
And you don't seem to bother this year!

Rachael Hammond (14)
The John Bramston School, Witham

Witchcraft

They think we are evil
With our pointed hats and black cats
But we think of love, candles
Altars and incense
As we cast our spells
The fog grows dense
Look up at the moon above
For it shall reveal your true love
Next time you see the stars in the sky
I want you to look up
And wonder why!

Sandy Rotondo (12)
The John Bramston School, Witham

Winter Wonderland

A winter wonderland with
The fluffy snowflakes coming
From the sky, settling down
On a tree's branches

Sitting by the fire with
A cup of hot chocolate or soup
Putting our feet up
Nice and cosy

The animals hibernating in
The woods, the hedgehogs
Squirrels, rabbits
And badgers

There's ice all around
It's like a slippery slug
So be careful
You don't fall over

It is cold outside
Put on those hats, scarves and gloves
To keep the warm in
And the cold out

When you go outside
It is gloomy and misty
If you can't see, be careful
You don't trip over

Christmas is here
Let's open our presents
See what we've got
To please us this year.

Bethany Vale (12)
The John Bramston School, Witham

Why Go There?

S chool's like a little brother you never wanted
C os it's boring, stupid and pointless.
H as always got something to get you in trouble for
O ur parents believe their word over ours,
O bviously hates you.
L ie through their teeth.

S ometimes I just want to run away.
U sually I just want to hit someone
C os I get so annoyed.
K icks you while you're down.
S chool really sucks.

Mark Brown (15)
The John Bramston School, Witham

Love

I love him loads and loads
My love becomes stronger every day
Especially when he notices me or even looks at me
I'd love him to love me back
I love him so much, I can't even open my mouth to talk to him
But when you love someone like I love him, it's hurtful inside
I don't think I will ever love someone like him again
Not even close, not even a little bit.

Corinne Fory (12)
The John Bramston School, Witham

Life

Life is just weird
It's just like a beard
It's all tangled and mangled
But sometimes it's nice
Just like when you're hot and jump in ice
But sometimes it's bad and you feel really sad.

Jamie Wallace (12)
The John Bramston School, Witham

A Poem About The Things I Like And Hate

S chool, something I really hate, but I have to go to get an education
A nimals, I really like animals, they're so sweet
R ubbish, I hate it, it makes everywhere messy
A vocados, I really hate, they're horrible, they taste really disgusting
H ome, somewhere I feel safe, home with my loving family.

Sarah Flood-Powell (15)
The John Bramston School, Witham

Hockey Is . . .

H ardworking
O ppositions are rough
C ompetitive
K eeps you fit
E nergetic
Y ou keep your eye fixated on the ball.

Sam Field (13)
The John Bramston School, Witham

Year 9 Is . . .

Lying on the beach on a sunny day.
Eating hot Chinese on a cold day.
An old, mushy tomato squashed on the floor.
A glass of cold, fizzy Coke on a boiling hot day.
Riding in a limo going to a concert.
Spending time with my friends outside of school.
Swimming with dolphins in a tropical ocean.
Snorkelling underwater looking at the coral.
Exams and revision.
Staying with my sisters during the holidays.

Ruth Taylor (14)
The Leventhorpe School, Sawbridgeworth

A Soldier's Story

I quivered as I climbed aboard
The boat which was going to take me to war,
It seemed to stare at me,
Swallowing all the joy I had experienced,
The wind harassed me
As I plucked up the courage
To wave and blow a kiss
To my family who I'd dearly miss.
My little boy chuckled,
I just put on a brave face, hoping,
Just hoping, that he and my wife would survive.

Amongst the muddle of men,
Grew uncertainty and fears,
Some too hard to imagine,
Others as simple as can be,
Though inside, before all the sunken thoughts,
Left pride for England,
Royal Britannia ruled every man's heart,
As they tried to cope and move on.

Shouting echoed in my ears,
Followed by screams and cries,
Spitfires danced in the air like ballerinas,
But inside was pain and hope.

Sand flew in the air,
Young men brutally killed,
Laying sorrowfully in blood-smothered sand,
Dreadful goings on around me,
Was like a stabbing in the back,
Wondering what the next day would hold,
Wondering if our dearly beloved England
Would win the war.

Holly Whitbread (12)
The Leventhorpe School, Sawbridgeworth

Year 9 Is . . .

Year 9 is being hit in the face with a snowball.
A yummy tub of chocolate ice cream.
The taste of Brussels with your dinner.
The bubbles from your Coke going up your nose.
A walk in the park with shoes that give you blisters.
Snuggled on the sofa chatting to a friend.
Walking my dog in the rain.
Laying on a white sandy beach with the hot sun shining on me.

Sian O'Connor (14)
The Leventhorpe School, Sawbridgeworth

Year 9 Is . . .

Being locked out in the pouring rain
A bag of stale pick 'n' mix sweets
A bowl of cold baked beans
A glass of fizzing, ice-cold Dr Pepper
The noise of helicopters flying over
Shopping and spending too much
A baby kangaroo jumping across the field
Flying out to Barbados and it rains all the time!

Amy Wilson (14)
The Leventhorpe School, Sawbridgeworth

Year 9 Is . . .

My face turning blue with the cold
The sourest sweet in the bag
As disgusting and soggy as a sprout
As fizzy as the fizziest can of Pepsi
Noisy as a landing helicopter.

Charlotte Fereday (13)
The Leventhorpe School, Sawbridgeworth

Year 9 Is . . .

Being struck by lightning
A tasty chicken burger
A plate of uncooked fish
The beautiful taste of Tesco value cola
Driving a Nissan 350z and overtaking everyone on the road
Playing with a cute little rottweiler
Lying on a sunny beach
When chips are called French fries because they're not, they're chips.

Bilal Mirza (13)
The Leventhorpe School, Sawbridgeworth

Year 9 Is . . .

Like being hit in the face with a snowball
It's like eating Chinese with loads of vegetables
A glass of apple Tango
A motorbike with no engine
Winning a motorcross race or losing like a worm wearing
Y-fronts, living in a bin
A chat with Dan!

Tom Buitenhuis (13)
The Leventhorpe School, Sawbridgeworth

Year 9 Is . . .

Year 9 is a big, cold, icy snowball
It's a big yummy tub of ice cream
The nasty taste of fish in your mouth
The fizzy tingle of lemonade on my tongue
The gorgeous beetle whizzing past in the street
The horrible rain that floods the floor
But the thing which I love the most is
My wonderful, lovely daddy.

Georgia East (14)
The Leventhorpe School, Sawbridgeworth

Year 9 Is . . .

Sunbathing in the hot, sunny weather - when we get it!
A piece of Galaxy chocolate melting in my mouth!
Being forced to eat disgusting Brussels sprouts!
Sipping on ice-cold Coke out the fridge!
Cruising down the road in the back of your mum's soft top car!
Walking the dog on a warm summer's night!
Sitting in my room doing *too much* homework
And listening to my music!

Vicki Lockwood (14)
The Leventhorpe School, Sawbridgeworth

Being Year 9 Is . . .

Being rained on, even when the sun is shining.
A fine piece of cake.
The last piece of food in the back of the fridge.
A smooth milkshake.
A ride to remember.
The best television show.
The softest bunny.
The girl of my dreams lying next to me in my bed.
A stab to the heart.
A hug off my girlfriend, Erin.

Joshua Horrax (14)
The Leventhorpe School, Sawbridgeworth

Year 9 Is . . .

A windy day in a classroom
Eating pizza in the dinner hall with my friends
Horrible mushy peas on the side
A nice can of Sprite
A classic old Mini Cooper zooming past on the way to school
Going home to my dog
Going back to Gambia to see my friends
Sitting in English getting really bored
And finally seeing my mum when I get home.

Alex Plummer (14)
The Leventhorpe School, Sawbridgeworth

Year 9 Is . . .

As scorching as the sun.
As sweet as scrummy Haribo.
As tasteless as Brussels sprouts.
Fizzy as WKD.
Driving in a dream hummer.
Winning a special dance competition.
Slippery as fish lips.
Beautiful as the Caribbean.
Nasty as spiteful girls,
But then happy like talking to my mummy!

Lucy Parker (14)
The Leventhorpe School, Sawbridgeworth

Year 9 Is . . .

Being snowed into an OAPs' home,
A burnt pancake with no sugar or lemon,
A can of baked beans which have been left open for weeks,
A hot Pepsi Max which has been left in the sun,
Watching a Kawasaki zoom past without you,
Getting hit in the face whilst boxing a brute,
A cat, soaked, cold and abandoned,
Uptown New York, empty and lonely,
A swarm of killer bees, buzzing and stinging,
Seeing a brother get hit or attacked.

Jamie Alison (13)
The Leventhorpe School, Sawbridgeworth

Year 9 Is . . .

Rolling around in the snow
A hot Chinese in the middle of the night
Eating dates with my nan
Becoming hypo with Red Bull
Cruising around in my brother's car
Coming home and climbing into bed
A multicoloured chameleon
People taking the micky out of my big wacky ears
Floating around on my way to Mars
Spending some alone time with someone I love.

Daniel Atkins (14)
The Leventhorpe School, Sawbridgeworth

Sea Weather!

The sea's weather changes all the time,
One minute it's dark then it's fine,
Shining and bright,
The sky was full of light
And when it's all clear,
It will suddenly disappear
And the rain and lightning will come,
The storm has just begun.
As the lightning strikes the now darkened sky,
All the waves will crash and cry.
Then will come the hail and snow,
The waves will rise like yeast in dough.
The thunder deafening your ears
And the waves crash against seaside piers.
The sea is a roller coaster ride,
In these waters many people died,
Then the waves will start to descend
And this storm will come to an end!

Hannah Rawlinson (13)
The Sweyne Park School, Rayleigh

The Sea Poem

A pleasant breeze is blowing,
The darkness begins to fade,
People are slurping ice cream,
Children with buckets and spades.

The sea is calm, yet vibrant,
Smashing against the stones,
The crowd are swimming calmly,
Towards the bright red cones.

The tawny sand blows,
Swirling with the wind,
The day is soon to end,
The sun is about to dim.

Georgia Vasa (12)
The Sweyne Park School, Rayleigh

Buffalo

The herd of buffalo is a volcano
Ruining everything in its path
Trees and bushes get trampled
The ground is barren in the aftermath

Like a volcano
The dust rises high
Glance all around you
It's fill the sky

The ground would tremble and shake
Very similar to an earthquake
Animals scatter to avoid the herd
The only safety is by being a bird

They twist and turn
And gather pace
You cannot tell
Who's winning the race

The herd is slowing
Almost to a crawl
Like a volcano's lava
Covering all.

Lilli Weekley (12)
The Sweyne Park School, Rayleigh

Arsenal

Lehmann, Almunia, take your pick,
Henry and Pires showing off their flicks.

Cole, Arsenal or Chelsea make a decision,
Jermaine Pennant was caught drink-driving and he went to prison.

Pascal Cygan is good in the air,
He's a bit ugly because he hasn't got any hair.

Sol Campbell is as strong as a rock,
You'll end up on the floor if he gives you a knock.

Francesc Fabregas is only seventeen years old,
He's always wearing long sleeves, he must be cold.

Arsene Wenger has been given sixty million to spend,
Henry wears his socks over his knees as if it's the trend.

Vieira is the captain of Arsenal and France,
Gilberto loves to samba dance.

Kolo Toure comes from the Ivory Coast,
He isn't one of those players who likes to boast.

Arsenal, what a team,
Watching them is like a magical dream.

Luke Horton (13)
The Sweyne Park School, Rayleigh

The Malogi Monster

The Malogi Monster lives in the sea
And he eats small children like you and me,
He has big black eyes and yellow teeth,
You wouldn't want to meet this fearsome beast.

But there was one person who braved the danger,
This boy's name was Tanny Major,
But he never came back,
All people found was half his backpack.

The Malogi Monster lives on his own,
All he wants is someone with him at home,
But no one wants to be with him,
They just want to kill him and put his bones in the bin.

So this is the story of the Malogi,
Now let's all sing ging-gang-gooli.

Paul East (12)
The Sweyne Park School, Rayleigh

Chips

Don't like them skinny, don't like them fat
I've never really liked them, that's for a fact

They stick to your mouth and make it all dry
My mum makes me eat them, I never know why

The smell of them cooking fills the air
I hold my nose, at dinner they're there

I sit at the table feeling so sick
Looking at my plate at the yellow sticks

My dad comes into the kitchen and stares at my plate
I tell him to take some and not to wait

Some people like them, you may agree
But skinny or fat, they're not for me!

Sinead Pretty (13)
The Sweyne Park School, Rayleigh

Trees

On a warm and sunny day
Somewhere I like to be
Is out among a shady wood
Looking at the trees
The branches are so peaceful
Just swaying in the breeze
The sunlight shines through gaps among the
Gently whispering leaves

What really does upset me
Is when trees get cut down -
Just to make more junk mail
To clutter up our town
Because it's mostly rubbish
We don't want anyway
I think it's time they realised,
Allowed the trees to stay

Although I'm anti junk mail -
There's nothing I like better
Than hearing from an old friend
When she writes me a letter
Another thing I like to do
Is sit and read a book -
And when they're from the library
We can all take a look

Trees can be so useful
To make furniture as well
Wooden things can last for years
When they have been made well
I think trees are beautiful
Of blossom, leaves and wood -
But may they only be cut down
For making something good!

Jasmin Wetton (12)
The Sweyne Park School, Rayleigh

Double Faced

He is the bright sun,
He is the sweltering heat,
He can come from anywhere,
Taking away your heartbeat.

He cracks and hisses,
Leaves blackness behind,
Causes mayhem and distress,
Leaving haunting thoughts in your mind.

By nature he can be an innocent baby,
His warmness spreading all around,
He lets you prepare food to eat,
Giving good ideas without even making a sound.

He can be a glimmer of hope,
That keeps on getting higher and higher,
He can be a friend or enemy to all,
You've guessed it right, yes, he is double faced . . .
Fire!

Julia Sood (13)
The Sweyne Park School, Rayleigh

Water Stream . . .

The water stream is a slithering snake
Making its way swiftly
Going for its own sake

Flowing upwards
Flowing down
Creeping up on you
Without a sound

Shockingly cold
Slipping so quick
Its rough skin
Is so thick

Could easily shock
With one small bite
Some are terrified
But it should be alright

Could wrap you so tightly
Until you can't breathe
Or make you feel cold
Just so you'll sneeze!

Li Sa Choo (12)
The Sweyne Park School, Rayleigh

My Mum

I love my mum so much, she is a kind and funny one,
She loves doing poetry and loves having fun.
The best thing of all - she is a very good cook,
She cooks the greatest pancakes,
Without looking in the recipe book.

She is a very intelligent and loving mum,
That's why I love her so much.
She loves us all so very much,
And has got the magic touch.

My mum is brilliant,
She is the best mum you could get.
The one bad thing about her,
Is that she snores when she's in bed.

I would still love my mum,
If there were any bad things she had done.
She is so warm and snugly,
And very cuddly,
That makes her the best mum.

My mum is beautiful,
She has short blonde hair,
It's so soft and beautiful,
And very, very fair.

I love my mum so much,
I really, really do.
She has made my life full of fun,
And made my family's too.

Jade Ryan (12)
The Sweyne Park School, Rayleigh

Hiding

And the hand is now the terror in front of me

    Hiding
    Hiding like me
    Hiding
    Hiding like me

I run away from the terror in front of me

    Hiding
    Hiding like me
    Hiding
    Hiding like me

It's too late
And his fist is now ready
It's too late
And my knees are not steady

    Hiding
    Hiding like me

Long dark hell and the hands come over me
Long dark hell and the horror is all I know

    Hiding
    Hiding like me

Help
Help
Help

Another day
In my violent world

Bang

    Continually

Smack

    Persistently

Pain

    Relentlessly.

Laura Watkins (14)
Thurstable School, Tiptree

Love . . . Good Or Bad?

And the things that I feel effect the decisions before me
Numbness

Numbness
Numbness inside
Numbness
Numbness inside

The feelings I have make my eyes deceive me

Numbness
Numbness inside

Every other thing
Seems to fade away

Despite what happens
Always wish to stay

Numbness
Numbness inside

Long strange future don't know where it will end
Long strange future don't want to know the end

Numbness
Numbness inside

Both have to try to make it work
Both have to try to make it work

Numbness
Numbness inside

Argue, angry

The sadness is drowning me
Completely overwhelmed and sudden depression

Numbness
Numbness inside

Want the world to open up
And slowly trap me

Hate
Hate
Hate

And the feeling is suffocating

Numbness
Numbness inside

Cannot agree, end up debating
The feeling is fading, the love is cremating

End
End
End

It was the last of this, there would be no more waiting

Hate
End
Love

Were the feelings inside.

Sarah Baker (15)
Thurstable School, Tiptree

Two Paupers, Two Snobs

Two paupers waiting for a bus at 6am,
In rags on their way to a hard day's work.

Two snobs in designer clothes,
A man in a dark suit with a diamond ring
And a young woman in an elegant dress,
Piled high with bling.

Two paupers crowded on the bus
Holding onto the handles, swaying from side to side.

Two snobs on their way to a shopping spree in London.

Two paupers up since 4am with bright smiles on their faces,
Ready and happy to earn an honest day's work.

Two snobs step out of their car, their faces as white as ghosts,
As they step out of their car they look like flamingo
Getting ready to glide through the crowds of London.

Zoe Willis (14)
Thurstable School, Tiptree

One Cool Kid In Detention, One Boffin Kid In The Science Lab

Waiting in the art class
One minute till the bell
A huge paper aeroplane
Flew across the room

The teacher
In an ugly linen suit
With short, brown hair
Yelled across the class
'Detention! Detention!'

The cool-looking boy
Leaning back casually on his chair
Like a gangster
Sat there laughing with his mates

Bring, bring, the end at last, or was it?
The scraping of stools made the teacher cringe
The cool kid stayed behind
Writing on the blackboard
Back hunched like Quasimodo

Meanwhile, next door the science lab was empty
Apart from one lonely child
Short hair, huge square glasses
Known as *the boffin* to the other kids

Grabbing a shiny test tube
And placing it upright in a rack
He then poured liquid into it
Splish, splish

Twenty minutes later
Two doors opened
Two doors closed
Two boys exited the school

The boffin and the cool kid
Brushed past each other
The end of another
School day.

Rory Youngs (15)
Thurstable School, Tiptree

Monsters

Closed in your room,
Every night,
Sitting and waiting for the day's light.

Your feet hanging over your wooden bed,
Waiting for the green, hairy beast
To pop up his mouldy-like head.

Make it go away,
Make night turn to day.

Waiting for the dark shadows,
Behind your bedroom door,
Waiting for the monster's fat and large claws.

Make it go away,
Make it go away,
Make night turn to day.

Thudding on the stairs,
Wondering who is there,
Could it be those two monsters who you call Mum and Dad?
The monsters that make your life unbearable and sad.

Make them go away,
Make the monsters go away,
Make night turn to day.

Carla Spenner (15)
Thurstable School, Tiptree

Alone

And she feels alone in a big crowd

alone
alone again
alone
alone again

she goes unnoticed hiding her identity

alone
alone again

she tries to blend
to avoid confrontations

she tries to blend
to hide her emotions

alone
alone again

long dull day and another one follows
long dull day and a whole week follows

alone
alone again

stuck in a bubble
her life is a misery

stuck in a bubble
her life is a misery

alone
alone again

she runs home
and the day's nearly over

face in pillow
and cannot stop crying

alone
alone again

she gets up
and looks at a picture

a smile
a smile
a smile

it is a rarity

alone
alone again

she paints in a book
she's painting her troubles

going away
and a great weight is lifted

paint
paint
paint

and the sadness is going

now
to
sleep

and a new day has broken.

Sian Fahie (14)
Thurstable School, Tiptree

A Scruffy Ex-Pupil In A Truck, A Well-Dressed Teacher In A Lexus

At the stoplight waiting for the light
    3.30pm on the back streets of Tiptree

A dark and rusty truck
    With a father and son in tatty overalls

Sitting with no emotion on their faces
    One of them fiddling with the 25-year-old radio

The other one staring into the Lexus
    Where the well-dressed teacher was lighting a cigar

The teacher in a silk pinstripe suit
    With dark spiked-up hair
Sitting on his seat as he was sitting on a bed of nails
On the way to his 5-bedroom stately home

The father and son tired
    Up since 2am repairing train tracks
        Oily and scummy from their work

The father with a crippled left hand and bloodshot eyes
    Looking across like an owl with its beady eyes
        The son with glasses which are nearly broken
With the same looking hair as the teacher

Now both father and son looking . . . gazing into the car
    Giving out vicious looks to the teacher as if he was an evil killer

The teacher scanning his satellite navigation
    Like it was a boring story in a newspaper

And the very red light for an instant
    Holding the three close as if there was a force present

And between them all across the small damaged road
    These people with completely different lives
        All wanting to get to their own palace.

Home.

Paul Wilding (15)
Thurstable School, Tiptree

Mum

Seven o'clock and the alarm goes off
I roll over and out of the bed
Drowsily eat my breakfast
And my mum bustles in
Handbag over her shoulder
Lipstick in her hand
Then out of the door
Leaving it to blow closed in the wind
Why can't I be a
Grown-up!
Grown-up!
Grown-up?

Eight o'clock and I'm leaving for school
Messy hair and baggy uniform
Bet Mum's at the bingo hall
In her skimpy dress and massive heels
She'll have another manicure and
Be out all night
I'll get another ready-meal and one more detention
Why can't I be a
Grown-up!
Grown-up!
Grown-up?

12 o'clock and I've got no lunch
Mum forgot to pack it, again
I'm sweaty from PE but Mum's in a limo
She just texted me with her brand new phone
I really, really want to go back home
I got beat up for being out of fashion
I'll need a new coat but I haven't got the cash and
Mum just bought a new leather jacket
Why can't I be a
Grown-up!
Grown-up!
Grown-up
And send *Mum* off to school?

Sophie Sheppard (14)
Thurstable School, Tiptree

Drugs

Injecting the poison into your veins

Don't do drugs
Drugs do damage

Letting that beautiful flower eat up your mind

Don't do drugs
Drugs do damage

You want to give up but you can't face the facts
You're wasting your life, you are under attack

Don't do drugs
Drugs do damage

Your self esteem starts to dissolve into darkness

Don't do drugs
Drugs do damage

You now start to realise you're a heart-empty addict

There's no going back!

Taison Wade (15)
Thurstable School, Tiptree

The Bully And The Victim

As the lunchtime bell rings,
The playground starts to fill,
Filling, filling,
Like a glass of water,
Into groups of popularity.

The newbie enters,
Confused like a newborn parrot,
No one wanting to talk to him,
For fear of rejection.

A bottle flies through the air,
'Heads!' the sound of the bully echoes round the playground,
The feel of pain as it slams against his face
And he falls to the ground.

A fierce shadow falls over the boy,
He has been in this position before,
At his old school and the one before that,
Then he realised that you can never escape
The vicious circle that is, the bully.

James Wren (14)
Thurstable School, Tiptree

Terrorism

And yet again our world is on top of me
Terrorism

Terrorism
Terrorism is around me
Terrorism
Terrorism is around me

As I look on, death is surrounding me
Terrorism
Terrorism is around me

Lives are ruined
Broken hearts

Lives are ruined
Suffering starts

Terrorism
Terrorism is around me

Planes crash and the ruins are crushing me
Planes crash and the ruins are too heavy

Many people die
And the terrorists are selfish

Many people die
And the terrorists are selfish

Terrorism
Terrorism is around me

People are injured
And they are going through pain

Terrorists die
And it is for their own fame

Terrorism
Terrorism is around me

Death
Death
Death

And the death cloud is black

Terrorism
Terrorism is around me

But there is hope
And the future is round the bend

If we work together
Terrorism would soon end

Peace
Peace
Peace

And there would be no suffering

One
Step
Closer

To a world of happiness.

Daniel Hume (14)
Thurstable School, Tiptree

Beggar In The Alley, Lawyer In The Street

Awoken by the sound of the drowning traffic
7am, Liverpool Street
Tall, dark, giant-like man walks so casually past
While the dirty, scruffy, tired-looking man attempts
To get up from the most uncomfortable night of his life
Sleeping on the streets, nothing but a ragged old jumper
And his little old dog as his only companion
The tall, well-dressed man looks down at him from a
                                      great height in disgust
Can't believe how he's spending his life
Alone on the streets, nothing, no money, no one
Just stars, frozen, wants to do something
Just hasn't got the heart to delve into his pocket for a
                                      couple of pounds
The beggar looks at him for a chance
A chance to be free, free with money, a job and a loving family
A family to hold him, love him and cherish him.

Phillipa Casey (14)
Thurstable School, Tiptree

It's Not Humane

And the intimidating chair fills the way in front of me
It's not humane

It's not humane
And it shouldn't take place
It's not humane
And it shouldn't take place

My body's now paralysed as the fear takes a hold of me
It's not humane
And it shouldn't take place

Nothing can be done
As the guards grab a hold of me

Nothing can be done
As I start walking slowly

It's not humane
And it shouldn't take place

I see the chair and it starts getting nearer
I see the chair and it starts getting clearer

It's not humane
And it shouldn't take place

I've been found guilty
But I haven't done anything

I've been found guilty
But I haven't done anything

It's not humane
And it shouldn't take place

I look at the clamps
Which will soon be holding me

The generator's on
And the current is rising

It's not humane
And it shouldn't take place

The generator's on
With the current still rising

Down
Down
Down

As I slip into the chair

It's not humane
And it shouldn't take place

I start to feel the cold
Of the clamps that are holding

I'm rooted to the chair
As the clamps are still holding me

Up
Up
Up

And the generator's ready

Long
Slow
Zap . . .

Chris Webber (14)
Thurstable School, Tiptree

Black And White

And a sea of people standing in front of me
Black
And
White

The waves were violent, crashing in front of me
Anger
Pain
Devastation

The racist remarks
Hitting people hard

The racist remarks
Breaking people's hearts

Discrimination
Prejudice
They're nothing but racists

All hope has been lost
Will they ever get along?

All hope has been lost
Will they ever be able to forget and move on?

Everybody is the same
But they are all too blind to see

Everybody is the same
But they are all too ignorant to see

Discrimination
Prejudice
They're nothing but racists

Nothing
But
Racists.

Jessica Colegate (15)
Thurstable School, Tiptree

Broken Man

He is different in so many ways I can't describe,
After killing all my kindred, he still repents to hide,
I tend like him but must destroy him just the same
And he inflicts on me an awkward kind of pain.

It crushes, eats, decreases and compels,
My soul and all emotion I would ever wish to hold,
All that is left of the man I once was,
Has been eaten into this death walking; what you see before;

You.
Kill.
You.

He will not live alone in his rich repulsive ways,
He will be a saint by day and then will choose to save,
All his antics and all that he may have done,
His ways are so unlike mine savour one.

Unlike me, a crippled dead defenceless fool,
He will not stop for mercy, he will always end the kill,
He vindicates and causes men to go insane,
All that is left of me is dead, calling in vain;

Help me.
You.
Help.

Now I will always end my task clean and free of pain,
He ended lives of everyone whom was held dear,
I see revenge on him to kill defeat and watch,
As all he will have left will fade and start to rot.

The problem with this whole debate is one which I must hide,
The story, saga, tale and legend ties up the only hitch,
The man whom I hate so much is concealed inside of me,
The broken man who I am, that broken fool is me.

Oliver Winn (15)
Thurstable School, Tiptree

Miracle

The two selectives are in front of him
Education
Drugs

He understands how much he can achieve
Education
Drugs

The choice of education is very weak
Like a mouse's tiny voice that is always outspoken

But still he knows how well he can achieve
And what a success story he will be
Education
Drugs

The choice of drugs has a power so imposing
Like the stench of a skunk
And the peer pressure being called from
His mates like a bunch of laughing hyenas

Education
Drugs
Drugs
Education

The scale is clearly tipped, but
A miracle is near

A teenager saying
Yes to education
And
No to drugs
That's a miracle.

Sam Webb (14)
Thurstable School, Tiptree

Crossroads

Opposite each other waiting to pull out, 7pm down Tiptree Heath
Huge, dirty, white van with three gypsies sitting in the front
One man, one woman, one child
Each without seatbelts and messy hair and clothes
A mud-sprayed caravan linked onto the back
Looking straight into the eyes of a family of four
Sitting on cream leather seats in a BMW
The man with 'blinging' ring
Holding onto the steering wheel like a woman holds a handbag
The woman so casually staring at her newly manicured nails
And sitting in the back, two perfect little girls
Hair in plaits and frilly dresses
The gypsies packing since 4am to make yet another home
The child with one ear pierced and shaven head
Bare black feet in the window
The woman shouting with her huge rounded mouth and greasy skin
Slamming her hands down on the child's feet
The BMW being awaited by a well-dressed man to open the gate
A gap in the traffic
And straight away the BMW pulling out
With no regard for the van
But for one moment, two cars so close together
Who in society
Are miles apart.

Jess Redfern (15)
Thurstable School, Tiptree